CHANGE
If I Can, You Can

Travis Angry has a remarkable story to tell, a drive to help our young people get through their struggles, and a faith and dedication to God that is inspiring for us all. His story, *Change: If I Can, You Can,* is interesting and engaging – a true role model for our youth to follow.

—**Cory Gardner**, United States Congress

You can't help but be captivated by the story of Travis Angry. He doesn't hold back as he confesses to the base emotions that have the powerful potential to destroy any one of us. As he rises to overcome his own demons, we learn how far the strength of faith and family can take us. This is a glimpse into the attitudes that fail and those that triumph as we share the walk of Travis Angry and his personal quest to be a better man.

—**Cathy Carlat**, City Council, Peoria, Arizona

In light of the recent tragic events in Arizona, Colorado, and Connecticut, ***Change: If I Can, You Can*** is a relatable story for youth and adults alike. I highly recommend this book to people looking to make a difference through positive change.

—**John C. Vitt**, CW5, GS, AZ ARNG,
Command Chief Warrant Officer

Travis' story personifies the American ideals of self-reliance and perseverance. His deep faith in God gave him the strength to overcome some incredible odds. Younger generations face a complex world that will test their ability to succeed. Anyone who reads this book will know even the tallest obstacles can be overcome with faith and a resolve to never give up.

—**Lieutenant Commander Ray Fryberger**, United States Navy

Change: If I Can, You Can, is an autobiography of difficulties, drama, and determination. Travis' story is a journey that youth, parents, and those who love and care for our youth will rejoice in, identify with, and find 'hope, through. And, hope is the foundation of the change that transforms inabilities to ability, dysfunction to function, and losing to winning! A 'real story', a 'real journey' of struggle, and a 'real life changed to be a change mentor for others.

—**Naomi Rhode**, CSP, CPAE, Past President National Speakers Association, Past President Global Speakers Federation, Co-Founder SmartPractice

Every generation for eons has looked to its youth for energy, intellect and progress. Many people feel this may be the first generation of Americans less well educated and motivated than their parents. Is anyone doing anything about this predicament? Yes –Travis Angry with his book and personal appearances. The most powerful role model is one who has most recently overcome the adversity faced by many American youth. Travis connects and his audiences correct. Given enough time and exposure, Travis will be an important influence on the next generation of working Americans.

—**Don and Kathleen Thoren**, Professional speaker, singer, coach and counselor, Speaker Hall of Fame, Author of personal and organizational success courses

This book is inspiring and thought-provoking. Readers of all ages will appreciate how God has worked in Travis Angry's life to mold him into a mature father and leader.

—**Lorri Allen**, broadcaster and author of *It's All Good News*

Travis shares from his heart the road of a young man who decided a life misunderstood wouldn't be his excuse for being a failure. He now stands strong in the midst of life's daily trials serving God, raising his two small children and pressing toward his passion for helping others.

—**Meg Britton**, Colorado Springs, CO

Travis Angry's story is incredibly inspirational. Walking through the darkness of circumstance, Travis helps us all understand we can join his mission of being positive no matter where we are now or where we've come from. I applaud his work, and look forward to seeing how this message infects a generation in need of a role model like Travis.

—**Andy Braner**, CEO/KIVU,
Internationally recognized speaker, author, and teen advocate

Change is a beautifully written, transcendent story of self-discovery, self-discipline, and personal growth. It will be an inspiration to everyone who reads it; and for many, it will be the epiphany that changes their lives for the better.

—**Clint Bolick**, Vice President for Litigation, Goldwater Institute,
Co-Author, *Immigration Wars: Forging an American Solution*

This book is a must read, from the moment I started reading it I could not put it down. This is a story that explains how perseverance PROVES to be the life blood to success.

—**Aaron Borders**, Current candidate for AZ Legislature,
Current Government Affairs Representative for NAIFA of
AZ West Valley, Financial Specialist and Risk Management Auditor

CHANGE
IF I CAN, YOU CAN

Changing for
the Better in You

TRAVIS ANGRY
Founder of the Change: If I Can, You Can Project

with Wendie Davis-Grauer

NEW YORK

CHANGE IF I CAN, YOU CAN
Changing for the Better in You

Disclaimer: The Publisher and the Author make no representations or warranties with respect to the accuracy or completeness of the contents of this work and specifically disclaim all warranties, including without limitation warranties of fitness for a particular purpose. No warranty may be created or extended by sales or promotional materials. The advice and strategies contained herein may not be suitable for every situation. This work is sold with the understanding that the Publisher is not engaged in rendering legal, accounting, or other professional services. If professional assistance is required, the services of a competent professional person should be sought. Neither the Publisher nor the Author shall be liable for damages arising herefrom. The fact that an organization or website is referred to in this work as a citation and/or a potential source of further information does not mean that the Author or the Publisher endorses the information the organization or website may provide or recommendations it may make. Further, readers should be aware that internet websites listed in this work may have changed or disappeared between when this work was written and when it is read.

ISBN 978-1-61448-649-7 paperback
ISBN 978-1-61448-650-3 eBook
Library of Congress Control Number: 2013933439

Morgan James Publishing
The Entrepreneurial Publisher
5 Penn Plaza, 23rd Floor,
New York City, New York 10001
(212) 655-5470 office • (516) 908-4496 fax
www.MorganJamesPublishing.com

To buy books in bulks, please send request to:
Travis@TravisAngry.com or call 623-451-4966.

Photographer:
Travis Angry, Inc.

Cover Design:
Mullins Creative, Inc.

Editor:
Jocelyn Godfrey
jocelyn@spirituscommunications.com

Interior Design by:
Bonnie Bushman
bonnie@caboodlegraphics.com

In an effort to support local communities, raise awareness and funds, Morgan James Publishing donates a percentage of all book sales for the life of each book to Habitat for Humanity Peninsula and Greater Williamsburg.

Get involved today, visit
www.MorganJamesBuilds.com.

Habitat for Humanity®
Peninsula and
Greater Williamsburg
Building Partner

DEDICATION

This book is dedicated to my mother and father:
Raymond Angry, Ph.D., and Glenburnia Angry, Ph.D.;
To my children:
Tatiyana, and DeVante;
And to my brothers:
Raymond Jr., Dexter, and Jason.

"It doesn't matter which way in life I go.
Either way, I win, because I'm a Christ follower."
—Dr. Raymond Angry, Sr.

TABLE OF CONTENTS

	Dedication	*ix*
	Author's Notes	*xiii*
	Acknowledgments	*xv*
	Preface	*xix*
Chapter 1:	The Beginning	1
Chapter 2:	Lost	22
Chapter 3:	Honor & Service	42
Chapter 4:	Health	58
Chapter 5:	Family	76
Chapter 6:	Education	106
Chapter 7:	A Message to Parents, Educators, and Community Members	123
Chapter 8:	If I Can, You Can	137
	Epilogue	*149*
	Appendix	*153*
	About the Authors	*167*
	Sources	*169*

AUTHOR'S NOTES

Twenty-two years ago, I made a big life mistake. The loneliness I felt was overwhelming. However, I didn't possess the desire to open up and share with anyone about the issues I was facing. My family didn't understand, and neither did my friends. I hid my heartache.

Choosing that route didn't prove profitable. Looking back, I think about what my adult self would have told my young, adolescent self. I imagine the conversations that would have taken place had I not wandered down such a rough road.

I'm a big believer in the adage "everything happens for a reason." For that reason, my story is like my skin—I wear it, naked and unashamed. I accept it. It's mine, and a part of me.

Additionally, I embrace my story because I know it is something *you* can relate to: struggles, disappointments, and the feeling that you can't measure up or that no one understands. Maybe *you* are struggling at school and want to give up on education. Maybe *you* are that fifteen-year-old girl who just discovered she's pregnant and needs support. Do *you* have a rough home life? Are *you* trying to decide if you should deal drugs for extra cash to help your mom pay the bills? Dilemmas.

Hang-ups. Uncertainties. We all have them, and we have to face them and deal with them head on.

There *is* a solution, young people. There *are* people who care. *I care!* The ***Change: If I Can, You Can*** project is reinventing our youth culture. It is bringing a voice to the adolescent who feels he or she doesn't have one. It is becoming the bridge that uses love to overcome broken homes, alienation, and lack of respect.

Throughout the struggles you will read about in this book, I have learned one important lesson: The biggest key to being successful is to *not* feel ashamed or devalued. Adults and our youth culture need to work together to right these negatives. Resources *are* available for you, even if you are a young person who feels caught in the middle. For example, counselors at your schools or churches can help you deal with the issues that plague you.

If you are an adult reading this, I'd like to exhort you to this point: Communities need to rally around one another. *We are all in this together.* The ***Change: If I Can, You Can*** Project has other resources in the works. The ***Change*** Project will continue to build toward the creation of a film, a magazine, youth conferences, and dinner galas; we welcome you to take part! I believe that when our communities succeed, so will this nation.

I'm on board, folks. I respect you and care deeply about what you're facing. My heart is open, and you've got my listening ear. I don't want you to be whisked away by the clouds of helplessness or hopelessness. Contact me anytime via Twitter (Travis Angry) or by email at Travis@TravisAngry.com. I'm here for you. ***Change: If I Can, You Can*** is on board. How about you?

ACKNOWLEDGMENTS

First and foremost, I would like to thank the Lord for His love, grace, and direction in my life. To my amazing parents, the late Drs. Raymond and Glenburia Angry, thank you for raising me with love and discipline; I will work tirelessly to continue the legacy that you left me to follow. To my children, Tatiyana and DeVante, you are Daddy's inspiration and motivation to make the world a better place. Thank you also to my brothers, Raymond, Dexter, and Jason—I love you all dearly. Thank you for being there for me through the ups and downs of life. To my entire family in the Bahamian Islands— Samantha, Cecil, Auntie Florine, my late grandmother (who taught me the value of the Bible), my cousins, and many others—thank you for your continued support and love. Thank you also to the entire Angry family whose roots have taught me to value life and strive to accomplish my heart's desires.

Thank you to the brave sailors I served alongside on the USS Kitty Hawk and Fighter Squadron, 192 Golden Dragons. Thank you also to the US Army National Guard and US Army for a second opportunity to wear the uniform proudly. To the best NCOs, 2-12 Infantry Regiment of 4th ID, Fort Carson Army Base; and all of my commanding officers and senior enlisted leaders of the military; our country is great because of you.

A special thank you to those who played an integral part in my health and healing: the Miami and Phoenix VA Hospitals; Carlos Robles, M.D., my first oncologist; and his staff— Joseph Salvatore, M.D., Thomas Kummet, M.D., and their team of professionals who provided outstanding care. To Thomas Miller, M.D., and his amazing team at the University of Arizona Cancer Center in Tucson, Arizona, thank you for partnering with the Phoenix VA Hospital to ensure the success of my overall health. (Because of all of you, I am now half Sun Devil and half Wildcat.)

Thank you to CCV—namely Pastor Don Wilson and his wife Sue Wilson; current and former staff; and my CCV neighborhood small group, especially Lt. Commander Ray and Amy Frybreger, Randy and Bobbi Reed, Chris and Christa Ottersberg, and Tricia Westlund and family. Your support, love, and prayers have meant so much to me. To my home church of Miami, Church of God of Prophecy, thank you for aiding me in my spiritual walk during childhood. Bishop Herman H.E. Dean, your messages still impact my life. Pastor Noward and Ruby Dean and family—thank you for being a continued blessing. To the institution that has given me hope, inspiration, and knowledge—the University of Phoenix—as well as my professors and classmates, thank you.

I also am grateful for my amazing and creative team at *Change: If I Can, You Can.* Without you, none of this would have been possible. Please accept my deepest sincerity and gratitude for your time, talent, and friendship: Amy and Jordan Photography; Cailean CPA & Business Consultant, PLLC; Mullins Creative, Inc.; my stylist, Erika Johnson; Jeremy and Michael of Six Vine Media; Connie Mableson, my entertainment attorney; and Laurie Bird, my former assistant. Thank you also to three, talented ladies who made this book come to fruition: Sunday Panzavecchia, thank you for taking the reins in the beginning and hearing my story. You have become a great friend, and I love you so much. Wendie Davis-Grauer, my writing partner, thank you for taking the thoughts of my heart and truly giving this book project your all—you did an outstanding job. To my editor, Jocelyn Godfrey Carbonara of Spiritus Communications, Inc., thank you for teaching me, guiding me, and believing in my story from start to finish; your hard work and time was amazing. Thank you!!

Thank you also to David Hancock and the entire Morgan James Publishing team—Rich Frishman, Margo Toulouse, Bethany Marshall, and Terry Whalin—for believing in me, my story, and the power of change.

Thank you also to Lynn Wiese for introducing me to Morgan James and being a great consultant and friend. Thanks to my book PR/ marketing firm, Smith Publicity Inc. —Dan Smith, Sandra Poirier Diaz, you believed in me from *hello*; thanks so very much, you both have given this book life and an opportunity to grow and impact other lives. Also, thank you to Jon Ringquist of CAA, a great friend and mentor to my career. A special thanks to my family law attorneys—Jennifer Wright in Phoenix, Arizona, and Tony Ditommaso in Chelan County, Washington. And to my good friends, ShaRon Rea and Debbie Blackmon, I owe you tons for your great friendship and love for the kids and me.

To the other awesome people who have touched my life in more rewarding ways than I can count: my spiritual mom, Meg Britton, your guidance is immeasurable; Jennifer Crotty, thank you for helping me start anew in Arizona; the Still Family, especially Tom, you've been the greatest friend and your story will be told soon, "deuce-deuce." To my Australian friend, Marie Ellis, your consistent love and friendship has allowed me to continue to grow; thanks for being my biggest fan. My dear friends, Lucas and Christa Atwood and Zach and Lisa Shepherd, and Ann and Jeff Carpenter your help and prayers are greatly appreciated. Desiree Gaston and my Dayzsha, who is like a daughter to me, keep striving to be great in making a difference. My Colorado friends, DeMarcus and Tiffany Hysten, thank you for your faithfulness and never leaving my side. A huge shout out to all my boys in Miami: Craig Pratt, Cary Felton, and Rajhan Smith. To Chad and Jennifer Tapscott, thank you for supporting me in my role as a father. To the Vistancia Community; my kids' school principal, Steve Gillett, and their teachers, Denise Koterman, Rachel MacDonald, and Kathy Ganem; your leadership and educating of our young people is valued.

To those contributors, readers, and supporters I may have failed to mention, please know your efforts and contributions do not go unnoticed. *Change: If I Can, You Can* is a conglomeration of people who desire to see our youth culture impacted in a positive way. Thank you to each of you who play an integral role in its success.

PREFACE

One of the most vivid and significant moments of my life occurred on a routine day. I was driving from my home in Phoenix, Arizona, the "Valley of the Sun," to the Carl T. Hayden Veterans Affairs Hospital for chemotherapy treatment. The sun's rays scorched the landscape and seemed to set the city on fire.

I mopped sweat from my forehead and cranked the volume on the car stereo to better hear, "I Can Only Imagine," by the Christian band, Mercy Me. Music flowed out of the speakers, and I hummed along in unison. This song had played a major role in helping me overcome my struggles, and gave me strength, hope, and the understanding that my place beyond this world would be amazing, and my future would be great. The lyrics served as a source of strength during difficult times and comfort throughout joyful moments.

The hospital lot wasn't crowded, so I parked, hopped out, and walked to the main entrance. After flashing my ID card to the security personnel, I gave a hearty hello to the veterans hanging out in the lobby. When I checked in, I greeted the same guys who sat in the waiting room every time I made this trip to the hospital. Though many of them had fought in the World War II and Vietnam eras and were in their sixties and seventies—and were quite a bit older than me—I considered some of them my best friends.

I know some young adults wouldn't even think to form a bond with anyone around their grandparents' age, but I've always found it a gift to be in the presence of mature adults. They have an infinite amount of knowledge to share with those willing to listen. In my case, I also think our military experience and our compromised health served as a bridge to close that age gap. The chance to sit in the adjoining cafeteria over eggs and grits with these guys before my treatment always made my experience more of a pleasure than a pain.

Being sick requires a lot of waiting in the lobbies of clinics and hospital rooms. For whatever reason, on this day, rather than taking a nap or thumbing through a magazine, I sat back and reflected on my life. I marveled at the extreme highs and lows: my troubled teenage years, dropping out of high school, my military experience, and my relationship with my family. Throughout every incident, there seemed to be one reoccurring theme: *change*.

I'm just an ordinary man who has had some difficult times, but no matter what happened to me, I always possessed the ability to better my circumstances. Struck with an epiphany, I asked the nurse on duty for a pen and paper and jotted down the most important phrase I'd ever written:

CHANGE
If I Can, You Can.

CHAPTER 1

THE BEGINNING

"Change does not roll in on the wheels of inevitability, but comes through continuous struggle. And so we must straighten our backs and work for our freedom. A man can't ride you unless your back is bent."
—Dr. Martin Luther King Jr.

Before you know who I truly am, I want you to know where I've been. Like many people, my life has been full of ups and downs, good times and bad. I've struggled throughout life in every sense of the word, and through trial and error, the path I am on now is the one I've been trying to steer toward all along.

In the cotton fields of Albany, Georgia, lies a place unknown to most—a place that I like to call "America's beautiful secret." It's a place where the sweet smell of peach trees fills the air and the warm sun shines endlessly. Even though my family (my mother, Glenburia; father, Raymond; and oldest brother, Raymond Jr.) only stayed until I was six months old, I consider Georgia to be an important part of my roots. My father grew up in Georgia and told countless stories about his childhood and my grandfather's funny cough (which I will mention again later!).

Of course, living in the South as a black man during the 1930s was not the most ideal situation. Some of my dad's stories took place during a few of America's hardest times: the Great Depression, the Civil Rights movement, and the Vietnam War. While growing up, my father and his family lived and worked on a Georgia plantation owned by a white family. Every member of the family—including my grandparents, my dad, my two aunts, and my three uncles—were expected to perform hard labor day after day. This included training horses, tending to the fields, and picking cotton. My dad spoke of being hunched over the cotton plants in the sweltering heat, day in and day out, trying to amass the one hundred pounds of cotton that would earn our family and him one dollar. As much as my grandparents wanted to participate in the Civil Rights movement, the family who owned the plantation where they worked would not allow it. They could have been fired...or worse. However, my grandparents did what they could to contribute to the "fight for freedom," often visiting church services to draw strength and guidance from the words of Dr. Martin Luther King, Jr., spoken through their minister.

Even though life was hard, my father's humble beginnings lit a fire inside of him to strive for something better. As soon as he was old enough to enlist, my father joined the United States Marine Corps as a means of escaping life on the farm. Later, my dad was drafted into the Vietnam War. Later, he was injured in battle when he was hit with flying shrapnel on his left side. Though weak from that injury, he considered his enlistment in the military to be one the best decisions he ever made because it allowed him to buy my grandparents their very first home for twelve thousand dollars. His decision to give my grandparents that gift and thus begin to repay them for all that they

> Even though life was hard, my father's humble beginnings lit a fire inside of him to strive for something better.

had done for him throughout his life was an example of his strong character trait of gratitude.

My father graduated from Albany State University with a BA in sociology. Later, after he married my mom, he obtained his master's degree in criminal justice. He was the first member of his family to graduate from college, and that gave him great pride. In his youth, he performed the work of a slave, but by the time he was twenty-three years old, he'd earned two college diplomas.

My father was a man deeply affected by what he experienced in life—both where he came from and the nature of his upbringing—and therefore developed a true appreciation for where his life was headed. As most people are aware, there are many incidents on life's path that bring moments of great change. For my father, one such change took place one month prior to his first college commencement. My grandmother, my father's biggest fan, died as a result of complications from diabetes. Her death rocked the entire family, but my father took her passing particularly hard.

When someone dies, people go through a natural cycle of mourning; but eventually, most are able to move on with their lives. Not my father. After his mother's funeral, my father sat at her grave, each and every day…for hours. He was so brokenhearted over losing her that he simply *could not* resume his normal routine. Eventually, my grandfather stepped in and *insisted* that he pack up and move to Miami, Florida, to be closer to his sisters.

My dad struggled with depression, not only from his mother's death, but also from the effects of war and the injuries he sustained. When he moved to Miami, he lived with his sister, Fannie Lue. One day, he told Fannie that he wanted to find a job. She told him she didn't feel as if he were ready to be employed with all that he was facing, but he persevered anyway and landed a job at Bakers shoe store.

One day while working, my father saw a lovely woman, my mother, enter the store. He asked if he could assist her with trying on shoes.

Through the course of their conversation, he quickly became enthralled by her and offered to purchase her shoes for her. "No, mon', I have my own money. I can buy my own shoes," she answered. Though she turned down his offer in her thick, Bahamian accent, their interaction must have made quite an impact because she invited him to visit her in the Bahamas sometime. From there, according to Aunt Fannie Lue, my father and his sisters would travel back and forth to the Islands while he courted my mother. My father loved to tell that story of how he met my mom. He liked to say that he fell in love the first time he saw her and refers to their July 24th, 1971, wedding date as the highlight of his life.

Though my parents met in Miami, they really began married life together in Georgia. They had my brother, Raymond, in 1972, and I followed suit in 1974, right before my family relocated back to Florida.

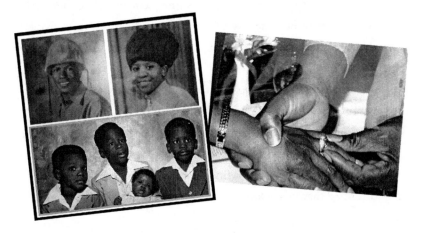

Despite the fact that my father wished he could have given his children the gift of a Georgia upbringing, the reality of emotion tied to his mother's vivid memory would have been too difficult for him to bear. Often, my father would comment that the love from the women in his life and my mother's act of introducing him to a belief in God were the only things that brought him through that dark period.

My parents shared a bond unparalleled by many other married couples. In fact, if one of them went into the hospital for treatment, the other one slept by the bedside until discharge, at which point they both emerged from the automatic doors, hand-in-hand.

I didn't always appreciate my parents' close and rare bond. Like most children, I would often butt heads with my mom or dad and run for support to whichever parent I didn't happen to be fighting with. Without fail, my parents would always back up one another. At the time, I would yell, "You only love each other and not me!" before storming off in a huff. However, what I didn't realize at the time is that my parents were giving me the greatest gift any parent could ever give a child: the gift of a strong marriage and a unified front in parenting. By teaching my brothers and me that a husband and wife should always love and be supportive, my parents were providing us with a sense of security and trust in the power of love.

If there was a poster child for "best mom in the world," my mother would have won, no contest. She fit this phrase to a tee. Her life was devoted to two things: God and family. In fact, she was so unselfish that she held off entering her career as a nurse until she had raised her four sons. Her faith gave her a strength that made her seem impervious to adversity, and it was a source from which she drew endless amounts of patience.

I remember one particular time when I was a kid, being a royal pain—whining and pouting because I was hungry. My mom was busy cleaning the house and didn't want to stop. I could easily have made myself something to eat, but everything always tasted better when Mom made it. I stomped into my room and slammed the door because I felt so heated with her. However, when I least expected it, Mom was at my bedroom door with a hot plate of food in hand that she had cooked just for me. Despite my behavior, as I mentioned before, she was the best mom in the world...

In general, my early years in Miami were good to me. Things were financially better for my family as my dad had found work as a public school teacher, and my mom had resumed her career as a nurse in a retirement home. I was becoming more aware of the world around me. I can remember to this day what a beautiful Miami sunset looks like—full of warm and radiant oranges, reds, and yellows. I remember playing in the streets, getting chased by dogs, and sitting on my dad's knee while he read the Bible. I was growing taller every day, and as I grew, so did my curiosity of the world. Often, I would turn toward my maternal grandmother from Nassau—my mother's mom, Epsie Lena Clarke—for answers.

When I asked, my grandmother told me about Jesus and God, and made sure to tell me about the difference between heaven and hell too. After she told me her spiritual story, my father's church showed a video following the same story line—only with very vivid imagery. The movie showed fire and people suffering. I got the point very quickly; seeing that at the tender age of six or seven made me realize that hell was not going to be an option for me. The film scared me to death! From that point on, I knew I needed to make it to heaven. My grandmother seemed to know so much about this topic, and when I asked her how she got to be so smart, she told me it was because of the way she was raised.

My mother's family originated from Nassau, one of the many beautiful Bahamian Islands in the Caribbean Sea. We would take a family trip and visit there every Christmas. Nassau was like a dream to me. The water that surrounded these islands was such a beautiful shade of aquamarine; I could have stared into it forever. I loved visiting because the different culture always made for a great adventure.

As far as raising children goes, the lifestyle in the Islands isn't like it is here in the States. As my mother would say best, "Children don't backtalk, they don't act up, and they don't look ugly; otherwise they'll get their faces knocked off their bodies."

My other favorite reason for visiting Nassau was my Auntie Florine who lived there. She was really my mother's cousin, but I referred to her as my aunt. Auntie Florine was another great woman in my life, not only because she knew how to cook explosive and flavorful "soul food," but because she believed in me, too. She would always stick up for me and tell everyone who doubted my dreams that I would make something of myself. In this life, everyone needs someone to believe in them, and Auntie Florine was one of those people for me.

While we were in Nassau, the whole family would have Bible study together. We would gather in a circle, hold hands, and pray. My grandmother's sister, "Sister Hattie" as we called her, would lead. She was an evangelist and had dedicated her life to the Lord.

These precedents formed the roots of my values and morals; but as I grew older, I tended to drift into my own routine.

Growing up in Miami was a lot of fun. Our family had moved out of a small trailer and into a house. I had friends to play with, and life seemed to be getting better all the time. We were living in Scott Lake—a small community in North Miami, Florida, that some would probably label a "ghetto" —but there was a great sense of community amongst the residents that outsiders looking in could not see. My dad would host these big parties at our house, and they would last all hours of the night. He was a dancer too. I used to watch Dad dancing in front of the big mirror in our living room. Man, could he get down!

One of my most vivid memories of Miami life involves Mr. Russell's barbershop. It was the place to be. That shop offered all the crazy hairstyles of the day, with designs and everything. Mr. Russell was married to a Spanish woman. This added to the comedic atmosphere that went along with the place, because she would get mad at him and tell him off in Spanish, and no one would understand what she was saying. Mr. Russell also had an area in his store where he sold shaved ice cream, soda, pig's feet, and candy…you name it, and he had it to sell. Finally, Mr. Russell's barbershop was the best spot to get up-to-date information. Anything you wanted or needed to know that pertained to sports, politics, or religion—you asked Mr. Russell or one of the many characters who frequented his place.

Though my dad looked at Mr. Russell's barbershop as a sort of "man cave" and enjoyed the everyday happenings that went on, a struggle was brewing inside of him all the while. He did his best to conceal his inward battles and have a smile on his face. Some days, however, Dad could be seen sitting in the corner of Mr. Russell's barbershop, in his own little world, while the rest of the group was engaged in whatever dialogue.

As much as my father had tried to defeat his demons by moving out of Albany, the pain of losing his mother grew to be too much for him to bear. Even though he didn't let the rest of the world know it, he was still in remorse over his mother's death months before, and would head straight to the local tavern after work. This was a place where he could drown his sorrows—where his constant companion, alcohol, never expressed judgment.

These drinking episodes happened many times when I was a kid; however, one night, in the summer of 1978, when I was just four years old, the cushy bubble that encased my world suddenly burst. I awoke from a deep sleep to the sound of my father stumbling through the house, knocking things over, and then to my parents' shouting. The door of my bedroom was cracked open. The light from the living room poured onto the floor, showcasing my parents' shadows darting aggressively, like some kind of horrific puppet show.

For a few moments, I was too frightened to move. My heart thudded in my ears as I listened to the madness just outside my door. Finally, I crept out of bed and reached out a trembling hand to shake my older brother awake. He did not stir, so I shook him harder. He still did not wake. As I listened to my mother plead with my father not to harm her, my desire to ensure that she was still safe overcame my fear for my own life. I crept toward the door and pushed it open wide enough that I could slide out into the hallway. What I saw next will remain with me forever.

My father stood in the middle of the living room, breathing heavily. I had witnessed my father intoxicated on previous occasions, but I immediately recognized that on this night, he had reached a new and terrible level of desperation and despair. His eyes were bloodshot and burned with a fury that was completely foreign to me. His massive build shifted from foot to foot, and he struggled to keep his balance. The pungent, sweet smell of alcohol burned in my young nostrils. Everything inside of me told me to run, hide under my bed, and cover my ears until morning…but it was then that I saw my mother crouched in front of him, trembling like a wounded hyena encircled by a pack of ravenous lions.

"Give me some money, Glenee!" my father roared, stumbling toward her.

"Please, Raymond, I ain't got no money!" my mother begged, her deep, brown eyes wide with fear. For some reason, her response infuriated my father. He lunged past her, yanked open the kitchen drawer, and pulled out a long, sharp, butcher knife.

The blade ominously glinted in the dim kitchen light before my father whipped his body back toward my mother and pressed the blade to her jugular. I blinked, hopelessly believing that I had imagined it. "Give me some money," he slurred again, slower this time, spewing venom with each word.

"Raymond, *please*. I told you, I ain't have no money," my mother pleaded in a trembling whisper.

She began to tumble backward, and my father moved with her in a sickening dance. As she attempted to navigate backwards, my mother's hands frantically groped behind her back, and she fell backwards over the leg of one of our dining room chairs, crashing to the floor! Still, my father kept the blade pressed to her throat. "Give me some money," he spit for a third time, now knelt over her, straddling her small frame.

I stood frozen in the exact same spot, trying to convince myself that what I was seeing was just a terrible nightmare from which I would soon awake.

But deep inside of myself, I knew I wasn't sleeping. "Please God, don't take my mama!" I silently prayed. The seconds felt like hours as they ticked by. And then, as though he had been aroused from his drunken state by some unseen, third party, my father dropped the knife to his side, roughly removed himself from my mother's body, grabbed his keys, and stormed out the door.

As soon as I heard the rough bang of the screen door, I bolted back toward the safety of my bedroom. My whole body convulsed as I let out heaving sobs, trying to come to grips with the reality that I had almost lost my mother, my world. But as I gathered up the courage to check on her safety, I heard passionate howling outside my door once again.

This time, the voice I was hearing was not filled with rage, but with fervency and hope. As I ventured out into the hallway again, I was greeted with the image of my mother kneeling in front of the couch, eyes closed, praying to God: "Lord, please help to bring me through this; bless my husband, help my family…" Her voice shook, but no tears streamed down her weary face. I had always known that my mother was a religious woman, but it was that moment that taught me the depths of her faith. My father had done something that would have broken many women. However, my mother's heart could not be broken because it belonged to God, making it forever impenetrable to defeat; and as the following days would soon prove, it was also open to forgiveness.

Even though my father had physically and verbally abused her, my mother's heart could not be destroyed. She'd been raised a Christian woman, and she knew that if she trusted her heart to Jesus, all would work together for good. Over the next couple of years, my father was able to draw inspiration from my mom's faith. He found his way to the Lord, and—through counseling from our pastor, prayer, and his own deep convictions—he also found change. Everyone who has ever struggled with a substance abuse issue knows that having people who stand in your corner and believe in your ability to heal is the best shot you'll ever have at getting better. Throughout everything, my mother never left my father's corner. She was like a healing balm to his soul, and that, along with God's help, ended up being his saving grace.

Through building his relationship with God, my dad found a new passion for serving and became able to overcome his reliance on alcohol. He began reaching out to those in need and preaching the gospel. Over the next several years, God worked vigorously in my dad's life to restore his heart back to a positive state.

This period marked several dramatic changes for our family. Despite my mother's fervent religiousness, we hadn't gone to church all that much in my early childhood. But now we attended church regularly, and our pastor, Bishop Dean, would come to our home and minister to my dad one-on-one. Eventually, my father even became a licensed minister in the Church of God of Prophecy.

When I was very small, I remember being in church in the summer of 1979. The song "Amazing Grace" came on. My dad jumped out of the choir where he was singing and ran to the back of the church, alive with the love of the Holy Spirit. I couldn't help but think of the man my father had been only a few short years ago, broken and beat down by disappointment and sadness. Now, here he was, healed by the love of God and his fellow man. Seeing my father's eyes change from being filled with rage and sorrow, to overflowing with love and passion, has been the greatest change one could hope for in a man.

Though "Amazing Grace" remained his absolute favorite song, my dad loved to sing Christian songs in general, and he could move thousands with his singing. He was affectionately known as the "James Cleveland of the South." My father was one of the lead singers in the South Florida Mass Choir, and they even recorded an album. He sang a song called "I Am Determined," which became a hit on the local gospel radio station in Miami.

Hearing my father's voice singing on the radio was such a joy. Even as young as I was, hearing that sweet song fill the rooms made my heart swell with pride. Though age and illness ravaged the power of his song in his later years, members of his congregation still would ask, "Dr. Angry, would you sing for us?" And of course, he did. Through the stories my dad told me about overcoming the challenges he had to deal with during his life, his path to greatness continues to be very encouraging to me to this day.

During the time period of reconnecting with God, my father used Dr. Martin Luther King, Jr., as his inspiration to better his life. One incident my father told me about often is the time when Dr. King was marching in one of his rallies and someone from the crowd threw a rock and hit him in the head. Though Dr. King was in a great amount of pain from this injury, it didn't slow him down. He just kept marching. The same thing happened to my father one day at the school where he taught. His students had always feared him, not because he was a mean guy, but because he was the principal. He was more than six feet tall, weighed three hundred pounds, and had lightning speed. Students would purposely skip school so they didn't have to deal with Principal Angry (no pun intended because of his name!).

One day, as my dad was monitoring the bus station at school and making sure all the students were getting on their respective buses, out of nowhere, someone threw a rock and hit him in the head. Luckily, he was okay. Even though he was shaken

> Never be afraid to work on a job. Whether you are working in a bank, teaching in a classroom, cutting someone's grass, or raking someone's leaves, do your job *to the best of your abilities*. Try to be the best banker, try to be the best teacher, or try to be the best at cutting someone's grass. However, beyond doing the best at your job, the most important thing is to get a good education in the process.

up a bit, it didn't prevent my dad from completing his job. Principal Angry took his duty seriously; there was nothing that would prevent him from completing the task at hand.

To this day, there is one particular conversation that my father had with some friends and me that still sticks in my memory. He sat us down at my house and said, Never be afraid to work on a job. Whether you are working in a bank, teaching in a classroom, cutting someone's grass, or raking someone's leaves, do your job *to the best of your abilities.* Try to be the best banker, try to be the best teacher, or try to be the best at cutting someone's grass. However, beyond doing the best at your job, the most important thing is to get a good education in the process. You will need a degree to succeed in our world. Go to college, and make sure you finish school, because in the long run, you will need it."

I would be lying if I said I never discounted my father's advice. Throughout my youth, I was always jealous of my brothers' successes. As they continued to achieve great things, I couldn't shake the feeling that I could never reach their level of accomplishment.

My brother, Raymond Jr., always seemed to have everything go his way. He was the oldest, so naturally he was accustomed to being first at everything: dinner, riding in the front seat, getting to sit next to Mom, and so on. Whenever I would complain about this, he would always shoot back, "Well, I'm the oldest!"

Raymond Jr. always excelled at everything from school to sports, but his real passion was music. Today, Raymond is a very talented piano player. As much as I love to watch and listen to him play, I would be lying if I didn't say his talent still has the power to make me a little jealous.

Raymond had always been a good role model for me and my two younger brothers (even though he use to kick my butt until the day I was bigger than him and was able to stop him from doing it anymore). My fondest memory of growing up with Raymond is when we would walk down the street and around the corner together to Mrs. Berry's house for our piano lessons. Mrs. Berry was the neighborhood piano teacher, and the most humble woman you could ever meet. She was also the choir director for the youth group at our church. Mrs. Berry was very passionate about helping her pupils learn about music.

Raymond Jr. was so creative and gifted with the piano that he was selected to attend New World School of Arts in downtown Miami. Not only did this impress me and the rest of our family, but his growing talent also served as a source of inspiration for himself. Raymond's gift at playing the piano inspired him to take up the keyboard, and from there he went on to learn the organ. His musical talent became a big hit at our church, which made him very popular. As much as I love Raymond, I can't help but acknowledge now that his overall greatness in every aspect of life contributed to my constant need for reassurance and attention in my own childhood.

As a teenager, the times of having no major responsibility began to fade, and life seemed to beat me down even harder. I found myself growing increasingly jealous of Raymond Jr., and that jealousy turned into envy when he received a musical scholarship from Howard University in Washington D.C.

When he arrived there, it was the first time he saw black kids his age with musical talent that matched or exceeded his abilities. The other kids had a different style—they played a different type of jazz and their music was fresh and expressive—constituting something that Raymond had never seen or heard before.

While studying at Howard, Raymond was a member of the college band, and was scouted by a talent agent who asked him to travel the country with the popular band, Shai. This was huge for my brother, and he couldn't justify passing up the opportunity. The next day, he broke up with his girlfriend because she wanted him to stay in D.C. with her. He used a limousine phone from a Los Angeles airport to call home and tell my parents the news.

Being that education was so important in my parents' eyes, they weren't exactly thrilled that Raymond Jr., the oldest son in the family, had dropped out of college to travel the country playing with an R&B band. My brother did everything he could to convince them that he had made the right decision, but it was a hard sale to say the least. In an attempt to make amends with my parents over dropping out of school, Raymond arranged for the money he was making to be sent directly to my father.

After about two or three years when the band's touring slowed down, my brother decided my dad was right and enrolled back into Howard University where he graduated and later went on to obtain his master's degree as well. However, his music career was far from over. It was always his dream to play on the main stage. He even played for President Clinton and President Bush, but knew in his heart that New York was where he was going to make it. So in early August of 2001, he packed a truck he rented and moved his life to the Big Apple. He was finally settled in the beginning of September 2001.

About a week after my brother had moved the last of his belongings into his apartment, the most dramatic and devastating catastrophe ever to happen on United States soil occurred.

Ironically, my brother had been performing in the North Tower of the World Trade Center at an early morning gig just two hours before the attack. Something told him that after breakfast he didn't need to go back. The people who needed to hear him play already had, so he tentatively concluded that he was done for the day and went home to catch up on his sleep. His roommate at the time, our cousin, later woke him up and told him what happened. Aside from disbelief, he was unharmed and continues to live in New York to this day.

In sequential order after me is my brother, Dexter, who I'm the closest with now. Dexter was always the funny one, acting goofy just to get a laugh out of his peers. He was also quick-witted and always had a funny joke to share. This aspect of his personality has carried over into his adulthood, as he now works as a professional comedian and has appeared at the Apollo and on VH1 and Comedy Central numerous times.

While he always had a sense of humor growing up, Dexter was generally pretty quiet and spent most of his free time playing video games. Even though I swore he played them all of the time, he managed to be the smartest of the brothers. He was even accepted to a magnet school, Miami Braddock High.

After high school, Dexter's brief stint in the United States Marine Corps seemed to really bring him out of his shell. I remember the first time I watched him do a stand-up routine. I was so nervous for him and didn't want to see him fail. He never faltered, the crowd loved him from the very beginning, and his comedy excelled more with time. Whenever I have seen him perform, he has always received an amazing reaction from the audience, no matter how big the lineup.

The cycle seemed to be happening again: First, my older brother experienced great success, and now my younger brother was following suit. To top things off, my father was awarded a promotion at work. Things were going well for everyone…except me. I was moping around the house, depressed, and unmotivated to change. My older brother had left me behind, my younger brother was passing me by, and I was beginning to think, "When will it be my turn to shine? When will it be my turn to have the attention?" Things naturally seemed to get worse when my youngest brother, Jason, was born.

I remember the first time I laid eyes on Jason. I woke up that morning in 1980, rubbed my eyes, and headed into the living room. That's when I first saw him sitting in his car seat, happily sucking on his little, dimpled fist. As I tiptoed closer, I thought he was beautiful with his light complexion. I bent down and stared at him for what seemed like ages. When he looked at me, I knew right away that I wanted to be a positive influence in his life. I made a promise to myself: I was going to be the best big brother I could.

But it was a promise that I did not always keep. Jason and I fought a great deal while we were growing up, probably because we were so much alike, both always getting into trouble. Unlike Raymond Jr. and Dexter, Jason never seemed to express any interest in education, making mediocre grades throughout grammar and high school. Today, he works as a chef for the Bank Atlantic Center in Sunrise, Florida, for the Florida Panthers Hockey Club; despite our best efforts to get him to look into college, he always refuses, saying it isn't for him.

Naturally, raising four boys was a tough task for my parents, especially for my mother. During the summers, it was extra hard for her—we were out of school and home with her most of the time while Dad worked. We would take trips to church conventions and youth fairs and even went to Disneyworld a couple of times. But my fondest summertime memories are from when we would head back to Georgia and visit my granddad, who, by this time, had married my step-grandmother.

I had a great relationship with Granddad. I used to sit beside him on the floor while he rocked in his chair, watching his beloved Atlanta Braves. He loved baseball, and that carried over to me. Even though he is no longer alive, that common thread still binds us today. Just recently, I attended an Arizona Diamondbacks game, and I swear I could feel him sitting there next to me, yelling at Jon Garland to strike out a player. He was always a very passive, kind, and humble man; but he could discipline like no other.

I remember one time while visiting him I made the mistake of cursing in Sunday school. (You know by now how religious my family is and how big of a mistake my cursing was.) Once, it got back to Granddad that I had used foul language in the one place you're not supposed to use it; he knew he had to take action. It was for my own good, as I recall being told, but it didn't seem so good at the time!

He brought me into the study in the corner of his house where he kept "the rope." Now, I'd heard stories about "the rope" from my dad and knew this wasn't going to be good. Even though I obviously didn't enjoy this, I found it sort of funny that my dad's story about my granddad's funny cough was true. You see, every time he would discipline me with that rope, he would cough, as if it would register in his head that him swinging that rope against my backside should warrant a cough in response.

Being the mischievous little kid that I was, I also caught my fair share of "whoopins" in general. When I misbehaved, my mom or dad would whip me on the butt with a belt or some other implement. And sometimes, in the grand tradition of Southern black discipline, I would have to cut my own switch from outside. In an attempt to be goofy in the face of punishment, sometimes I would come back inside and hand my parents a tiny twig. Of course, after they had a laugh, I would then have to go right back outside and fetch another one. As much as I know some folks feel as though this kind of punishment is cruel and abusive today, I always understood that they did it because they wanted me to mature into a disciplined, humble, loving individual who did not feel as though he could walk all over other people. As hard as my mom and dad tried to live an honest life and raise honorable children, they too are only human, and I witnessed them falter in their lives as well.

One summer afternoon when I was about thirteen, Dexter, Jason, and I were home alone. Mom and Dad were out with friends. We were watching TV in the living room when, suddenly, we heard glass shatter in the front of our house. Scared, Dexter and Jason ran out of the living room and into my parents' room. There's a joke in the black community that whenever danger is afoot, you ain't supposed to stop to investigate— you just run! However, my curiosity got the best of me, and I decided to go check things out.

I snuck into the kitchen and found myself face to face with a tall, black stranger wearing heavy chains around his neck. He looked me up and down and casually nodded in my direction, "'Sup, little man?" he nonchalantly asked, smiling to reveal gold teeth. My heart was pounding faster than it ever had, and I feared for my life. I back-peddled out of the kitchen and raced down the hall to my parents' bedroom closet where my brothers were already hidden. They had dialed 9-1-1 while I had been in the other room staging my grand investigation.

The police came a few minutes later and took us to Dexter's godmother's house. Luckily, nothing was taken from our home, but the burglar was never caught either. This incident really brought my brothers and me closer together and seemed to sew the gap that our typical adolescent quarrels had created.

Later, when my parents arrived to pick us up, my dad—being the supportive father he was—didn't want to harp on the incident too much. He didn't want his boys being afraid in their own home. However, the incident obviously affected my parents a great deal more than they let on, because immediately after the break-in, they decided to move the family out of the ghetto and into the suburbs. After many weekends spent house hunting, they finally settled on a home in the affluent suburb, Pembroke Pines, Florida. Our new home was a colonial two-story with four bedrooms and three bathrooms. The exterior was painted a soft peach. The front lawn was an amazing, tropical, Caribbean landscape with thirty-foot tall palm trees that you could reach out and graze with your fingertips if you were standing on one of the beautiful balconies.

Upon moving to Pembroke Pines, it quickly became apparent that the standard of living in this community was far from that of Scott Lake. It seemed like everyone here had a nice car, a big house, and expensive clothes.

With privilege comes expectation, and parents in Pembroke Pines *expected* their children to excel at everything. Bragging was the standard communication amongst parents. Soon, my parents seemed to be asking more of me. The demand for me to live up to my parents' newfound expectations was something I wasn't ready for, and I found myself unable to adjust. My grades in school started to suffer, I had low self-esteem, it seemed as if I couldn't do anything right, and my life was heading down the wrong path. I can remember test days at school when I wanted to ace them so badly, just so I could be on the same level as Raymond Jr., but it just never seemed to happen for me. I would get upset and lose all confidence in myself.

Furthermore, my father became over confident with his life. He acquired a new swagger mainly due to our "keep up with the Jones'" lifestyle, and this was beginning to give the wrong impression of what love meant. The simple things we used to do as a family didn't seem so simple now. Going to church was becoming a chore because my father seemed to be competing with other families—it wasn't about going and showing our faith; it was about who had the more expensive suit, or whose Cadillac had nicer interior. I didn't understand. Why was something we used to take pride in becoming such a hassle? This had a negative effect on our family and seemed to be sending the message that money could buy love.

Meanwhile, Dexter graduated from high school and enlisted in the United States Marines. My family planned to visit him when he graduated. My father was a proud papa because Dexter had followed in his footsteps of joining the Marines. I watched my dad that whole day; watching his face brought joy to the family. It is amazing to see sons following in their father's footsteps, and I was watching my younger brother do just that. We got a tour of the base; we saw the training facilities, sleeping quarters, mess hall, and even saw him march with his unit while wearing his camouflage uniform. I wandered around the base a little, just to immerse myself in this new world my brother was about to claim as his own.

Once we got back home, it hit me: my younger brother—my best friend—had left me. I was sad and headed towards self-destruction. I knew this wasn't good.

In fact, I was so depressed that soon I dropped out of high school. I didn't know what I was going to do with my life.

So there I was, twenty-two years old, living at home with my parents and my youngest brother, Jason. Meanwhile, my older brother was approaching graduation from college, and my closest friend—my younger brother, Dexter—was stationed in North Carolina. Once again, everyone's lives seemed to be falling into place...except mine. I was a mess. I had no self-esteem; I was a high school dropout; and to make matters worse, I was losing my relationship with God. I knew it was my turn to be the role model for my younger brother, but it wasn't happening. Jason and I were fighting all the time, and our relationship was turning sour.

I knew that I was not keeping my promise to set a positive example for Jason, and I wasn't giving my parents the respect that they expected and deserved. Something inside my heart kept telling me that I needed to go further, to explore the reasons why I felt the way I did. It was time to better myself...it was time for a change...

CHAPTER 2

LOST

"Our greatest glory is not in never falling but in rising every time we fall."
—Confucius

The path to righteousness took a long time for me to find. I wish I could say I kept my promise to Jason and myself, but I didn't. Growing up in Scott Lake was difficult—I always found a way to get myself into trouble at home and at school. One educator who always seemed to have it out for me was Mrs. Young, the assistant vice-principal at Hibiscus Elementary. She was a beautiful woman, about forty years old, but most students feared her because she believed in the "spare the rod, spoil the child," logic. In fact, Hibiscus students referred to her paddle as, "the butter from the duck," a Southern reference for discipline. Every time I was sent to her office, she gave me a whoopin' like no other!

When I was twelve years old, I attended Highland Oaks Middle School, and my best friend was Raheem Rivera. We lived in the same neighborhood and did everything together. At that age, friends are a kid's whole world; Raheem was definitely the closest person to me at that time.

I remember when I first met Raheem and invited him over to my house. My dad had built a basketball court in our backyard, and we played on it for hours. Basketball quickly became our favorite activity. Though Raheem was short—standing at five feet, three inches—he was quite the little jumper! I was about five feet, nine inches, but Raheem definitely held his own at the net.

I enjoyed attending middle school. Highland Oaks consisted of one large building, two stories high. The school was encased in stucco, pink as Pepto-Bismol. It housed a few thousand students, grades six through eight. The hallways of the school held the student lockers, each secured with a combination lock which we had to provide. Just like the connectors that these hallways were to the classrooms, I often thought that the transition from childhood to adolescence was similar— equipping each student with determination, responsibility, and the ability to walk through new doors of opportunity.

Yes, middle school helped with my development. I felt especially grown up at twelve years old because I was allowed to ride the city bus alone to school each morning. Before school started, my friends and I would gather at Scott Lake Park and play football. It was *the* place to hang out because all of the cute girls were there…making it a great way to start the day before the bell rang!

I had excellent classes and soaked up all the knowledge my juvenile mind could handle. My favorite class was history; I seemed to have a knack for understanding the material. Discussion of past wars, influential presidents, and various branches of governments caught my interest at an early age. I think I made the best grades in this class partly because my father taught history at nearby middle schools, Madison and Lake Stevens. Conversely, math was another story. Mr. Kennedy, a hard-nosed man (who definitely did not favor me), taught that class. However, Mr. Kennedy was a teacher who brought excitement to learning. He walked and talked with a certain air of sophistication, which intrigued both his male and female students. He looked a great deal like the stereotypical professor—thick glasses, elbow patches on his sweaters, and a confident swagger. It always seemed that Mr. Kennedy let the girls get away with a great deal more than the boys, but that never seemed to stop me from pushing his buttons.

I would make jokes about Mr. Kennedy, sometimes pointing out the obvious, which he did not always appreciate. Sometimes, he sent me to detention. Due to my behavior, I spent a lot of time within the four walls of a confined classroom, forbidden to talk with my peers and subjected to the slavery of class work. Detention was often the result of my tardiness, talking during classes, forgetting my homework—you name it, that was probably on the list as well. Sometimes my teachers would even call my house around dinnertime to let my parents know how poorly I was acting in school. Of course, this would always result in receiving a whoopin', so I eventually learned to disconnect the phone right at 5:50 p.m., listen obsessively to our phone messages, and delete any that might have incriminating evidence of my behavior.

The truth is that I wanted to be a first-rate kid, but I just couldn't figure out how to manage. It was like trying to find a foreign destination without a map. I desperately wanted to bring home straight As like my brothers had, except I was too busy trying to impress my classmates to dedicate enough time to studying.

> The truth is that I wanted to be a first-rate kid, but I just couldn't figure out how to manage. It was like trying to find a foreign destination without a map.

My overall favorite class was Mrs. Bassie's home economics. Not only did the cooking part of the course make me happy, but so did seeing the teacher's daughter, Shayla Bassie. I was falling for Shayla, hard and fast... she was a beautiful girl, with a tall, slim frame and light brown skin. Her chocolate brown hair reached to the middle of her back, and her huge brown eyes made me weak. Shayla was quiet, obedient, and studious: the opposite of me. I had taken an interest in girls by that time, but

Shayla was the first girl I ever really wanted to date. I liked her so much that I tried to memorize her schedule and "accidentally" pass her when she came out of her classroom. We had P.E. together. When class was over, I would stand by my locker and wait for her to come out of the girls' locker room just so I could see her face and watch her walk down the hall. I was only twelve, but Shayla was my dream girl. We would play the game four square together. I decided one day that I couldn't keep my feelings in anymore and wanted to express them to her somehow. I was too afraid to tell her I had a crush on her, so I told Raheem, in hopes that he would try and facilitate our young romance.

One winter day, our P.E. class was out on the field, and this random girl started chasing me, acting like she liked me. Out of the blue, Shayla came up to me and asked me for my phone number. I was in shock. *Finally!* I was able to pull myself together to get her digits as well. I called her that night and was giddy because I was talking to my dream girl!

Valentine's Day was just around the corner, and I couldn't wait to buy Shayla some balloons. It was my way of expressing my deep feelings for her. I will never forget when I saw her carrying them. *I was so happy...* but she never said thank you. It turned out, according to several classmates and news that spread like wildfire in our middle school, that Shayla *actually liked* Raheem. My heart was broken. That night, I turned on the slow jam radio station and cried myself to sleep thinking about her. My friendship with Raheem started to fall apart, and we didn't really talk anymore. It felt like I had done nothing wrong and still I lost my best friend and my girl. I became depressed. The situation really affected me, my grades, and my whole experience in school. Soon, girls became my number one priority. I thought I could *prove* that I was *worth something* if I could win over the hottest girls.

At this point in my adolescence, I started to realize the struggles that would soon become a constant pattern in my education. I knew I had talent, but I was more focused on being accepted by my peers than doing well in school. I was striving to be "top notch" for all the wrong reasons. I was searching for love in all the wrong places...probably because I did not feel love at home or within myself. Instead, I just felt like a disappointment to my parents because I wasn't excelling like my brothers. A tough war was waging inside my soul. I was envious of Raheem because he had Shayla. I desired to be more athletic and play for the basketball team. I also wanted to be smart like my brothers and classmates, but I seemed to fail at everything. I drifted into a negative pattern, and my already low self-confidence was eating away at me. Things were so awful for me, I contemplated suicide.

Many days, I would skip school and go to the mall across the street. I did not know whether I was coming or going in life. It was as if I were a lone piece of driftwood—floating in the middle of an endless sea going nowhere.

My parents were doing the best job that they could of providing for my brothers and me, but I was still lost in that equation. Raymond had his music, Dexter had academia, and Jason was still too young to have to worry about anything. It felt as though everyone in my family had a plan except for me. My grades were mostly Fs, and I did not possess the motivation to do my homework or study. Even though my father was a disciplinarian, I'd still rebel because I no longer cared about the repercussions of my actions. The beatings, and discussions that my parents tried to use to get through to me, were growing increasingly ineffective as I drifted further into my negative self.

On the days that I did go to school, I couldn't wait to get home and go to my neighbor and friend, Ricky's, so we could play pickup games of basketball. This helped to keep me occupied and out of trouble. God knows there were many opportunities for me to drift into drugs and alcohol, but I believe that He was watching out for me in this sense.

I remember when I encountered my first opportunity to smoke. I was walking from the bus stop to school and saw this guy smoking. I asked him if he had another cigarette. He handed me one without even really looking at me. Because of the morals my parents had instilled in me, I felt it was wrong for me to smoke. It took a few minutes of deliberation, but eventually I threw out the cigarette. I was proud of myself; I had overcame temptation and stayed strong. It was the first time I had really felt satisfied with a choice I had made.

Though it would have been an easy transition to begin drinking and smoking, I never picked up the habit. Disguised as a comforting companion, I saw alcohol as the nemesis it truly was—full of trickery and deceit. I remember how that lifestyle affected my father—turning my own flesh and blood into someone truly unrecognizable. Because of this, I promised myself at a young age to steer clear.

I know each one of us is confronted with difficult choices in life. With each decision, there comes a consequence. The most significant lesson I ever learned is that no one is defined by their choices; but rather, each person is defined by how he or she rises above the outcomes. I understood that if I tried smoking, it would open a door and change my life for the worst.

After that cigarette incident, I was getting ready to graduate from middle school and head to high school. In the springtime, our whole eighth grade class had taken a tour of North Miami Beach High, and I started to like the idea of going there. Even though I had a chance to attend a school closer to home, I chose to enroll in their summer session to try and get ahead, and then continue there the next year.

One day, I was hanging around after school, and I saw these dancers for the school band practicing. Amongst the dancers, I saw this girl, and found out that her name was Sandy Coffee. I had heard about Sandy from other students, and one look at her told me why. She was a sophomore and the most beautiful girl in the entire school. Sandy had an athletic figure, light brown skin, long, silky brown hair, and a perfect smile that lit up the room. Sandy's best feature was her eyes... hands down. They were caramel colored, and when I looked into them, I had to force myself to look away. Suddenly, little Shayla Bassie seemed a distant memory. I started to fall hard for Sandy.

My new school year was starting off well. I was doing better with grades, and that made both my parents and me breathe more easily. Thanks to Sandy Coffee, I even decided to join the school band. (My father had bought me a trombone one Christmas back in middle school. I had even played at my church, even though I didn't know how to play a single note or stay on key.) We would have band rehearsal every day after school, and playing at games was exciting and new to me. I was really enjoying the activities that came with high school life, and everyone seemed to offer me more respect because I was a band member.

Eventually, however, my newfound respect and the excitement of being a new student waned, as well as my resolution to better myself. I started to skip school again. My confidence was low, and I was not inspired. My only incentive for going to class was seeing Sandy or another attractive girl. My attitude was getting worse, and I started to head in the wrong direction again.

The fact that there was a mall directly across the street did not help my case. The mall security and management did not work well with school officials to keep us in class. It was a free-for-all, and I definitely took advantage of it.

My dad received phone calls about me not attending classes. I remember very clearly one time when my father showed up to school unexpectedly. I was already in the principal's office. My dad ended up giving me a whoopin', right in front of principal! Though it hurt, I had grown accustomed to his style of discipline…but it had little effect on the direction I was headed.

The only fixation I really had was Sandy Coffee. I told one of my friends about Sandy and how much I liked her. He tried to get me to go and talk to her, but I was too afraid. One day, I finally got that courage. Sandy was sitting alone in the hallway, waiting for her ride. My knees were shaking, and I thought I was going to wet my pants—but instead I walked up to her and said hello. She casually looked up at me, and I nearly swallowed my tongue when my eyes met her light brown gaze. I was lost in her beauty, but somehow I managed to ask her if we could talk sometime. She scrawled out her number on a piece of notebook paper and passed it to me without much emotion. I felt like a hero, and I had to resist the urge to dance back down the hallway.

My feelings for her grew daily, but I could not find the right words to express them again after that initial encounter. I did not know how to approach her. I was too nervous to call her on the phone. As a result, I ended up missing out in the end. My friend (who always tried to get me to approach Sandy) had actually used me in order to meet her. They ended up dating soon after I had asked for her number. One day, I found them kissing in the hallway. My heart was broken for the second time, and though I should have been accustomed to it, it was still just as hard as the first time. But, like that old saying goes, "the band must play on," …and I did.

I continued to play in the band, but it was mostly a social thing. Music was never important to me like it had been for Raymond. I also continued to skip classes. I would only skip once or twice a week, but it progressively worsened during my freshman year—that is, until I met Coach Balkman, the North Miami Beach men's basketball coach. He was about five feet, ten inches tall, with a husky build and a bald spot in the middle of his head. Coach Balkman also worked as a career counselor at the school and always managed to make time for any student who needed his help. After I met him in the career office, he quickly became like a second father to me. I think he could sense that I was a lost soul, so he had me spend a lot of time with him.

The school had an outstanding basketball team, and our best players were a set of brothers: Andre and Derik Taylor. Andre was older and arguably the better player, but he never did well in academics. He had a lot of school related interests, but his two favorite pastimes were women and partying. Like me, Andre's grades seemed to worsen with each passing term. Coach Balkman tried many times to set him on the right path, but those efforts were in vain. Andre ended up failing in many areas, which led him to drugs. I never heard anything more about Andre. However, his younger brother, Derik, was focused in school and went on to do great things with his life. He was the point guard for North Miami Beach High and ended up getting a scholarship to play college basketball at Florida International University in Miami. I even watched him play in a few games on TV.

Coach Balkman encouraged me to try out for the team during my sophomore year. When I didn't make the cut, I was crushed. However, he still wanted to help me to get out of my own way. He knew how much I loved the game, so he offered me a job as an assistant trainer. I was in charge of handling the uniforms, equipment, and water and towels—and helping with drill practices. It felt great to be part of a team and necessary to others.

During this time, I was still searching for who I was. I did a lot of things for attention. I longed to be noticed and yearned to be popular like the other kids. I stole more than a hundred dollars from my parents' bedroom, skipped school, and went to the mall where I purchased candy and more than thirty sets of balloons. I went back to school and passed them out to the most beautiful girls I could find. Some said thank you and gave me the most striking smiles; others thought I was weird and walked away. The overall attention I received made me feel good in the moment, but I soon realized the mistake I had made. Not only had I rewarded the girls based solely on their physical appearances, but I had stolen money from my parents in the process. That resulted in me going to desperate lengths that only hurt my parents and me in the long run.

My life at the time still had no direction. Soon thereafter, my father moved the family to the suburbs, and I was transferred to Miramar High. The opportunity for a new beginning brought high hopes. I remember my whole family walking through our new, beautiful home— me fighting with my brothers over who got which bedroom—and the thick, white carpet that lined the floors. I thought that this was going to be my chance to *finally* do good for myself.

I attended class and maintained a C average. I also wanted to be in the band. Miramar High was good for me at the time…until I amassed myself into the wrong crowds on the basis of wanting to be accepted. Seeing the school athletes with pretty girls made me want to have my own girlfriend. I tried so hard to meet and talk to girls, but it never seemed to work out. I didn't have many friends and would often eat lunch by myself in the cafeteria.

Things only got worse when Dexter came to school. I would watch him excel in his classes and develop new friendships while I became more isolated with each passing day. I felt invisible to everyone and the more I felt that way, the more I tried to act out and be noticed.

By this time, my schoolwork was starting to decline. I was no longer focused; other things took priority over my grades. I started to skip school once again, often going to a nearby friend's house. I was going nowhere, and my teachers and school officials started to recognize it. The possibility that I would even graduate from high school was starting to fade.

My relationship with my father was getting worse. We fought all the time. I had no respect for him. Instead of doing things to honor him like the Bible taught, I was doing the opposite. I was disrespectful to my parents by not coming home on time and refusing to attend church where my father would preach the Gospel. I showed no support—I was only focused on fulfilling my own needs. I found it a little easier to talk to my mother during that phase, but she always had the "no" syndrome, as in, "No, you can't go there," "No, you can't eat that," etc. As a result, I decided to make her answer a "yes" by default…by simply not asking.

One day, as I was watching a football game at our school, I noticed a tall guy wearing a Giants jersey, leaning against the bleachers a few feet away from me. He looked to be about my age, and I was flabbergasted when he came right up to me and asked me to hang out with him and his buddies. I was ecstatic that someone had finally reached out to me. I had a great time with this new group of friends. However, I soon discovered that this new group actually belonged to of one of the largest and most dangerous gangs in the United States. Still, I was so starved for love and attention that it didn't bother me. I even seriously considered joining the gang. The drugs they used every day didn't seem so bad anymore…but, in the end, I stuck to my commitment and never gave in to the use of drugs or alcohol.

Soon, my father and I had a huge fight in which he repeated what had become a daily refrain, "You're never going to do anything with your life, Travis. I am always going to have to take care of you!" Our argument escalated so much that my godparents came over to try and settle us. I was upstairs and wanted to leave, but my parents would not let me. I started threatening to jump off the balcony. In an effort to dissuade my intention to free fall, my godparents as well as my mom and dad tried to speak to me with love and concern.

My family ended up escorting me to a center in Miami for kids who struggled with emotional and mental issues. Everyone thought that something was wrong with me. Of course, I felt like I was okay, and everyone was just ganging up on me. I checked into the center and was given a room. I stayed for three months, including the Christmas and New Year's holidays. I felt so alone, even though my family did come to visit me a few times. I remember when Christmas came; I watched a family bring gifts to their son who looked to be about nineteen like me, and I started wondering what gifts my family would have for me when they arrived. However, when they showed up, it was obvious that they had brought me nothing. My parents made it clear that my Christmas gift was the money that they had spent on putting me in the center.

I can remember sitting in my room on December 31, 1993, waiting for the New Year to begin. At that moment, I made myself a promise. When I got out, I would finally change my life for the better. I was on a mission to make a positive change. I can remember the feeling when my parents arrived to pick me up. We were in the gym, and the feeling of walking out of that building was like walking out of prison. I felt like I had been given another chance.

The drive home was wonderful. I looked out the car window toward the placid Everglades and prayed that God would help me modify my behavior. It was the first time that I had prayed in years. When we got home, my mother fixed me a plate of her famous, Bahamian cuisine. By the grace of God, I had also lost touch with the gang I had planned on joining.

Sadly, however, going from the center's highly structured atmosphere to my unstructured life at home was too much for me to overcome right away. I felt overwhelmed almost immediately after re-enrolling in school. I struggled for the next few years to stay afloat, and I was ashamed that at the age of twenty-two, I was years older than many of my classmates. Soon thereafter, I made the decision to drop out.

After dropping out of school, I no longer cared about anything or anyone. I seemed to be falling back into the old routine of self-destruction. I felt worthless, and it felt like whatever I did, good or bad, didn't matter anymore. I stole my parents' car and got into an accident not too far from home. I had a friend help me push it home and into my garage. My dad was livid with me, but I really didn't care. I *did not* like to listen to people, I wanted to do my own thing, and listening to my family at the time was *not* an option. I was not being a solid example for my younger brother; he just watched me get into trouble all the time.

Ironically, the thing that ended up saving me from myself had been in my life all long.

At this time, I did not have a job and I wasn't going to school. I would often waste time meandering through my neighborhood. One day, on one of my walks, I noticed a park with a basketball court and a ball next to one of the hoops. I started playing, and was amazed at how good it felt. Playing basketball was the most favored pastime in my neighborhood. Every day for the next five years, I woke up and headed to Chapel Trail Park in Pembroke Pines where I played for hours at a time. Chapel Trail is where I met my buddy, Nick Marrezease, and we hit it off immediately. He was a kid, about sixteen years old, a lot younger than my twenty-two years. But at that time, I wasn't acting my age; I was acting like I was still in high school.

> Ironically, the thing that ended up saving me from myself had been in my life all long.

Nick and I hung out all the time, doing everything together including playing basketball, going to the mall, and watching games on TV. You name it, we did it. I met his family early on in our friendship. His mom was beautiful. She was petite with neatly styled blonde hair and kind, blue eyes. She was always in front of the stove, and she loved taking care of her husband and two sons. I loved her because she didn't judge me for my age, for being a high school dropout, or for not having a job; she only saw the good in me. Every time I would come over, she would make me my favorite meal: spicy chili topped with gooey cheese. She made me feel like part of the family. To this day, whenever I go back and visit her, she immediately places a bowl of that mouthwatering, roof-burning chili in front of me. In the wake of my struggle to identify my place in this world, Nick's family was a comforting haven.

My parents were struggling to figure out how to handle the son they didn't know how to help. They didn't want to give me more attention than my brothers just because I was acting out, and they resented that I was such a drain on their patience and resources.

By this time, my relationship with my father reached an all-time low. He decided to build a room within our three car garage by sectioning off a small space where I would live. He wanted me to make changes, and thought this could help.

By this time, my relationship with my father reached an all-time low. He decided to build a room within our three car garage by sectioning off a small space where I would live. He wanted me to make changes, and thought this could help.

He wanted me to partake in the process, but I wanted no part of it. I was uneasy about this; I felt like a leper, being cast out from the rest of the family. I felt more like an outsider looking in.

Once the room was completed, my dad would lock the entrance to the house, and I would have to stay in that room all day until he came home. He figured that while he was at work, I was not going to just sleep, play basketball, and watch TV all day long. I did not have a job, nor was I going to school; it was a sad situation to say the least. I desired to improve, but alas, I didn't know where to start. Getting out of the pit I

I desired to improve, but alas, I didn't know where to start.

trapped myself in seemed to be an impossible task. The room made me sad. I *hated* it—just like my father *hated* working in the cotton fields of Albany, Georgia. The space was the size of a jail cell, with room only for a bed and some clothes. There was no air conditioning, and the Florida heat was suffocating.

After I got out of my lockdown during the days, I ended up hustling people for money or rides around town, and going to nightclubs. I stayed out all night. I continued to just drift through life, but the troubles of my life soon caught up with me.

One night, Nick had invited me to hang out at my neighbor's house around the corner. My neighbors were away, and Nick had a female friend who was watching the house. There were about five people there when I arrived, and we all hung out and watched a movie. I didn't think much of it and went over to Nick house the next night as usual. His mom was not happy, as she had received a phone call that the police were over at the house where we had been hanging out the night before. According to the police report, something had been stolen. The police were looking for me, Nick, and everyone else who had been hanging out that night.

Scared as hell, I left and went home. When I walked past the street that the house was on, I saw all of the police cars. *THUMP! THUMP!* I felt my heart pound through my chest. I decided that it would be better for me to approach the police rather than have them come and find me at my parents' house. I was questioned along with the others. Then, Nick, the person who I thought was my best friend, turned to me and said, "Travis, why don't you just give them the jewelry you stole or tell them where it is?" I looked at Nick like he was crazy. I was shocked! It seemed because I was the oldest of the group and the only minority, those two factors were being used against me.

One of the policemen said, "Okay, someone tell us where the jewelry is, or we are taking everyone in." They gave us about fifteen minutes, and then the unthinkable happened. I was arrested along with Nick and Jim, but the girls were let go.

I tried to explain my innocence to the policemen, but they only chuckled and rolled their eyes as if to say, "Save it, Kid." I knew my parents were going to be furious, and I was right. My parents had warned me countless times that I was asking for trouble because of the group of friends I chose. Clearly, I did not heed their advice.

My father always told me and my brothers, "If you ever get arrested, I will not bail you out of jail; you are on your own. I did not raise you to get into trouble with the wrong crowds." I watched Nick's and Jim's parents come to the station to bail out their sons. However, when it came time to make my phone call, my dad repeated those very words to me.

> I felt so sad and alone. There I was, jailed for a crime that I did not commit...I sat there for days...which turned into months.

I felt so sad and alone. There I was, jailed for a crime that I did not commit...I sat there for days...which turned into months.

The food at the prison was horrible, and every day, I was forced to wear a hideous, orange jumpsuit. The other guys in the prison were in there for drug possession, assault, and robbery; I was frightened. Obviously, I wasn't a perfect kid, but I had never committed a crime. At first, I feared for my life—being amongst the hardened criminals with whom I was forced to eat, bathe, and sleep next to in the cell.

My cellmate was a big, bald, black guy who was jailed because he had beaten his wife. As the months wore on, we became close; often talking after the lights went out. He expressed to me how deeply he regretted how he had treated his wife. I poured a great deal of effort into convincing him that he could still do right by her. One night, he vowed that as soon as he was released, he was going to put his arms around his wife and never treat her poorly again. He remarked that she'd be shocked because he had never treated her well in the past. Soon, I extended my efforts to include

> I would often use the Bible to help convince them that it was not too late for them to change their ways. Knowing that I was helping others during my time as an inmate made the days a little easier.

several more guys in the prison. I would often use the Bible to help convince them that it was not too late for them to change their ways. Knowing that I was helping others during my time as an inmate made the days a little easier.

Finally, I received word that I was being released, and that I would not be going to court, as the charges had been dropped. My fingerprints weren't at the house, and the owners believed that I was telling the truth. My youth was coming to an end, and I knew I had to stop and think about which way I wanted my life to go. I knew right from wrong, but the decisions that I was making were hurting me the most. I vowed to make a sincere life plan.

One day, I saw a commercial on TV for Job Corps, a government-sponsored organization that helps disadvantaged or directionless youth ages sixteen to twenty-four find their niches in the job field. I immediately researched the organization, and found out that the nearest office was in Fort Lauderdale. After taking three different buses, I arrived at the Job Corps office, where I was able to sit down with a counselor who helped me settle on the field of retail sales. I wasn't sure where I should go, but I decided that I wanted to go far away so that I could start a new life for myself. I chose to study in North Carolina. After leaving the office, I felt great for the first time in years because I was finally allowing myself to understand that I was worth the effort.

Upon arriving home, I immediately told my father what I had done. He was skeptical at first, but it all became real to him when my plane ticket and other documents arrived in the mail. For as long as I live, I will never forget the day my father took me to the airport. On the ride there, he told me he was proud of me, and that he would miss me a lot. It had taken us so long to get to that point of mutual respect, and now that we had arrived, I felt like such a man.

Back in those days, you could actually walk with someone right up to the boarding gate of the flight. When I turned to walk down the corridor and board the plane that would take me to the next phase of my life, I felt someone catch my arm. I turned to meet my father's gaze, and I saw tears running down his face. He did not say a word; instead, he hugged me for a long time. I finally understood why he had been so hard on me all of those years. He so desperately wanted me to realize my own potential, and now that I had, our relationship was finally and forever altered.

My time at Job Corps was well spent. I worked hard and studied every day. For the first time in as long as I could remember, I made good grades and teachers did not despise having me in their classroom. I even made friends.

One night, we all decided to venture off campus and rent a hotel room for the night. There were several guys and girls from the program at the hotel party, and the liquor was flowing freely. I never drank anything; rather, I sat back and watched the others become more inebriated with each passing hour. What I was about to witness would change me. One of the younger girls was passed out on the bed, and I saw one of my friends start kissing her limp body. It was uncomfortable to watch, but I didn't want to start a fight with the guy so I just sat... frozen. Things got progressively worse, and soon the guy was raping her. After he was finished,

> What I was about to witness would change me.

another guy did the same. *I couldn't believe what I was seeing.* I felt paralyzed with fear and couldn't intervene. The girl was out cold, but what happened was so violent that her body jerked uncontrollably. It is an image that has haunted me to this day. After the party ended and we were driving back to the base, I knew that I couldn't accept what I had seen. I had to do something.

The very next morning, I waited in front of the director's office for him to arrive. Once he had, I told him every detail of the previous night. Immediately, pandemonium ensued as detectives and policemen were brought in to investigate. I received death threats from the very same guys who I thought were my friends. Still, I knew I had done the right thing. For my safety, the director decided to transfer me to the Job Corps in Georgia; but, before I left, the girl who had been assaulted found me on campus. She wrapped her arms around me and whispered through tears, "You're a gentleman, Travis, a true man."

For the longest time, I had felt like such a burden to others. To hear someone finally stop and tell me that I had positively impacted her life made me realize that I could never return to my old, negative ways. In fact, I became so inspired to do well for myself, that a new fire was lit in me. As a result of this newfound confidence, I even ran for student government eventually....

At my graduation from trade school two years later, I was asked to give a speech in front of a congressman, my classmates, and my family. I decided to speak about the power of change, and I used my tumultuous past as an example. When I finished speaking, the entire audience, including my father and Congressman Sanford, from Georgia's second congressional district, erupted into a thunderous applause.

After Job Corps, I worked with my cousin, Nate Benson, as an assistant at his music company. Nate was a manager of some up-and-coming recording artists, and he worked at WSVN 7 in Miami. His shift ended after the noon news telecast when he would come and pick me up at my house. We would go to events, rehearsals, or recordings. My cousin possessed some admirable talents within the music field, and I thought I could succeed in this industry as well. I worked very hard at shadowing Nate and soaked up all I could about the business. I even started my own record label called Set It Off Entertainment, though it never really got off the ground. My parents were proud that I stayed out of trouble, but they wanted me to go back to school. They thought that the music industry was a waste of time.

After much searching, I was able to find a job with America West Airlines, which allowed me to travel a bit. I liked many of the cities that I was able to visit, but my absolute favorite was Phoenix, Arizona. I loved how the intense heat would swallow me whole as soon as I stepped off the plane. I loved the cool rivers and the deserts that had been bleached white by the sun. I vowed that one day I would make a home for myself in Phoenix, but first I wanted to improve myself. I had become more focused than in my teenage years, but felt I still lacked discipline and leadership skills; so, I decided to enlist in the United States Navy.

CHAPTER 3

HONOR & SERVICE

"A life without discipline is a life without success."
—Travis Angry

I stood outside in the garage, looking at the "efficiency room" my father had made me call home for many of the past several years. I thought to myself, *"Never again will I live in this place… never again."* My eyes met my parents'—the look of surrealism on their faces confirmed the reality that life would never be the same. As we shared a tender and heartfelt goodbye, the doorbell rang. When I opened the door, there stood the man who would introduce me to my future. He wore the uniform that reflected the core values I hoped to possess: honor, integrity, courage, and commitment. To me, this man—Recruiter Williams—was the embodiment of the United States Navy. As we shook hands and greeted one another, I shifted my focus forward to where he was going to lead me, and I knew with absolute clarity I had made the right decision to serve. With that, we loaded my belongings into his vehicle, and off we went. I spent the night at the Days Inn Hotel in Miami.

I woke early the next morning, showered, and went to join the other military applicants for breakfast. We talked and joked, really just trying to get our minds off of what was about to happen. In spite of how much we desired to be sailors, we knew the biggest hurdles still lie ahead. It was October 31, 2001, and we were being shipped off to boot camp in Great Lakes, Illinois. While we waited at the Military Entrance Processing Station (MEPS), we were given our job assignments, picked up our bonuses, completed our paperwork, and received our official orders. During a lull, I replayed the phone conversation my parents and I had that morning. They told me they were very proud of me and my decision to join the Navy.

While on the bus ride to Miami International Airport, I thought about my father. We had been through so much together. I thought about the highs and lows of our relationship, about my dad's service to our country—his involvement in Vietnam combat—and me following in his footsteps. As I sat in the airport, my outlook was very noncommittal. My plan was to "just get by." I wasn't concerned about anyone or anything other than surviving the next nine weeks. As the plane took off, I knew there was no turning back.

> My plan was to "just get by."

After we landed safely at Chicago O'Hare International Airport, all recruits reported to the USO. We were given tags stating our names and where we were from. I scanned the room and saw people from all over the country—Hawaii, California, Arizona, North Dakota, and Wyoming; mine said, "Travis Angry: Miami, Florida." Then the words that made my heart beat fast were uttered, "Bus is here, load 'em up!" The petty officer in charge started calling names to load the Greyhound style bus that was emblazoned with the words UNITED STATES NAVY, GREAT LAKES, ILLINOIS on its side. I was called to board first because my last named started with the letter A. On the bus ride to the Great Lakes Naval Base, I was preoccupied with my own thoughts—

the military's expectations, drill sergeants, and how I'd react to physical training. *"I just want to get by these nine weeks..."*

When we arrived on base, my life changed immediately. The drill instructor jumped on the bus, yelling and screaming at us to get off his bus and into formation! This meant standing in the snow—in 20 degree weather for more than an hour. My hands were chapped, and my attitude was quickly going downhill. I wanted out—right then and there; no way could I do this for nine weeks! Alas, I had no choice. After our belongings were checked and we were searched by security, we loaded the bus again and entered the main gate. When we stepped off the bus, we were marched into the administrative building. The exterior was as cold and stone-faced as the drill sergeant. We were screamed at constantly. The petty officer lined us up against the wall—about one hundred twenty, would-be sailors, one right behind the other, noses touching the back of the next person's head. We stood in this formation for about an hour, unable to speak or move...if we did, we were yelled at by the officer in charge. This was the beginning of reprogramming our attitudes.

The drill instructor called off names, "Anderson, Andrew, Angry... *wait*, Angry? What is an Angry?" He shouted, "I have an angry man in my unit, hot damn! Angry, get down and give me twenty pushups...just because your name is hot and I love it!"

The petty officer continued to make fun of me and used my last name in idiosyncratic situations to get his point across—which he did countless times to "motivate" our unit. That was *the longest night* of my life. I felt like it was never going to end! We didn't sleep for the next twenty-four hours. Sleep was not even in our vocabulary. If we even mentioned the word sleep, we'd regret it because we'd receive an additional two hours of drill instructors giving us hell. By the time it was all said and done,

Sleep was not even in our vocabulary

we had been awake for forty straight hours. During that time, we had received our "welcome" into boot camp. Our "welcome" consisted of medical checkups, obtaining our uniforms and gear, being assigned to our units, and being marched into our barracks.

"Oh, let these nine week hurry and finish!" My attitude was my biggest challenge. Being a kid from the streets of Miami and then having orders barked at me minute after minute, hour after hour, started to get to me. I didn't care about anyone but myself; I just wanted to "get by." However, training was designed to reshape my mind-set. Because of my bad attitude and lack of motivation, I found myself completing more physical training.

Fatigue coupled with all the drill sergeants' shouting drained us mentally. We were also tested physically—running, pushups, chin-ups; you name it, we did it. However, one of my most memorable challenges was the swim test. (I remember thinking about how my dad looked at me quizzically one time in Miami and asked, "Travis, why would you join the Navy if you can't swim? What happens if your commanding officer tells you to 'jump ship'?" It was a comical moment that came to mind during boot camp and made me realize that if I was ever in that predicament, I'd better learn!) All the units were brought to the aquatic center on base, and the chief gave instructions. I will never forget his last directive. He said, "All those who know how to swim, step to the right. All those who don't know how to swim, step to the left." Everyone stood up, and all the white people went to the right, and all the black people went to the left. Everyone broke out in laughter; it was so funny. (Yes, I went to the left, went through some training, and eventually passed my swim test.)

My attitude went through different cycles. I went from "getting by" to becoming mentally engaged in challenging authority. The military was my daddy and what he said…went. At times, I also doubted myself. One day, my attitude got the best of me, and my drill instructor and I had a heated exchange. His constant badgering made me want to hit him. That would have resulted in severe punishment or being kicked out of the Navy altogether. Luckily, I realized that I had come too far to throw it all away.

Leadership stepped into the situation and detained me for one week. I had to get my attitude in check and back on track. After repeating the previous week's training, I was put into a new unit and given a fresh start. I had a newfound respect for my unit and leadership. I welcomed the training; I knew I needed discipline and direction in my life. I wanted to learn and become the best. I developed my own mission to aid me in the process. I told myself, no matter how miniscule a task, "I'm doing this for Jesus." If I was running, I would say, "I'm running for Jesus." If I was doing push-ups in the snow, I would say, "I'm doing push-ups in the snow for Jesus."

The Navy had ways of breaking people down and molding them into something new. Their habitual system ran pragmatically. The military was steadfast with their rules, and the only choice one had was to get on board. There was a precise way to do things, and this is something I resisted. For example, there was a certain way to fold a tee shirt. If I wasn't in the military, I would have taken that tee shirt, put it in a drawer, and not given it a second thought. If we didn't fold it correctly, however, we'd repeat the steps until it was satisfactory. In retrospect, this training—this learning about the rules—helped me with everything else in my life. It taught me to pay attention. It taught me to care, even about simple procedures. It motivated me.

When it came to motivating the unit, everyone knew "Angry" wanted to do it. I wanted to prove to myself that I could be the "great recruit." While doing physical training, I'd ask for more brutal exercises. This behavior made other recruits furious, however, because it only fueled the leadership. One time during our drills, the instructor brought in a carton of ice cream and placed it on a chair. He closed all the curtains in the room so as not to let in any light. He told us that we'd exercise until the ice cream melted. Something inside made me ask, "Is that all you got, Drill Sergeant?" The petty officer looked at my brazen disposition, called me over to the chair, and told me to sit by the ice cream. The next hour and a half resulted in rigorous regimens for the other recruits, while my drill sergeant made me relax. Needless to say, to express their resentment, I received *the beating of my life* by fellow trainees that night in the shower! Though it was difficult to ask for more painstaking tasks from those in authority, my newfound attitude allowed me to succeed in whatever the instructor threw my way.

I almost lost focus when we neared the end of boot camp. One day while in the chow hall at lunch, I was seated near the door where everyone returned their tray before exiting. A new unit came in, and my eyes beheld this drop-dead, gorgeous woman. She was Hawaiian, and I got lost in her beauty; I couldn't believe it. I had never thought I'd find good looking women in boot camp! Every time I entered the cafeteria, I would look for my "boot camp beauty." Each time, our gaze met for only a few moments, but we'd exchange smiles. This went on for weeks and was the motivation I needed to complete boot camp. Soon, it was time for the Captain's Cup games. This is where various units competed against one another and put all their physical training into practice. We were sitting in the gym, seated by unit, and hers happened to be next to mine. Though we didn't speak, we snuck glances at one another and smiled.

During boot camp training, the Navy forbids the opposite sex in different units to speak to one another. If we broke this rule, the punishment could be embarrassing. There was one point when a man and woman from different units were caught writing each other notes. The drill instructor wanted to make a point and use this as an example, so he ordered the female to read her note in front of the entire unit. It was humorous to all of us, but so humiliating for her that it caused her to break down and cry. That was her consequence for breaking the rules.

I thought about this scenario toward the end of the Captain's Cup games. However, when our units were getting ready to leave, this beautiful woman's belongings were right next to mine. I mustered up the courage to say hello. She said hello back. We exchanged a few words, and then I asked her name. She told me it was Hena Tapevalu. I didn't understand when she pronounced her last name, so she quickly scribbled down the name of her unit and her full name. I did the same. She then whispered, "Let's not get into trouble," so we went our separate ways.

I still looked for my "boot camp beauty." As we neared graduation, I badly wanted to see Hena. I knew I needed to focus on training and graduation—so I did. My focus was back on point, and I completed all my requirements. We then started to train for the graduation ceremony. Many times, I would stand there—thinking about how my parents were about to arrive for my graduation. I couldn't believe it. What would my father say to me? How would my mother feel about this achievement?

On graduation day, I got my answer as we marched in and came to formation. I could see my parents and my older brother, Raymond, in the stands. It was an amazing feeling to know that they were there in support of me. As I stood, I could see the look on my father's face, and it was evident how proud he was.

> The walk over to my parents and brother was the best walk of my life. This was truly a huge turning point in my life because I had received what I needed—discipline.

When the commander yelled, "Liberty call, you are dismissed!" I could taste the temporary freedom. The walk over to my parents and brother was the best walk of my life. This was truly a huge turning point in my life because I had received what I needed—discipline. I came to realize that it wasn't about me, and that my self-centered ways were gone. I wanted to help people and serve my country. My parents hugged me and told me how proud they were of me. My dad began to cry, and my mother couldn't stop smiling. My brother told me he was proud of me too. It was a great feeling. After graduation, we left the base and spent quality time together on liberty call.

Soon, the time came for my parents to return to Miami and Raymond Jr. to Washington D.C. I came back to the barracks and was bum rushed by a friend in my unit. He had a big smile on his face and told me that my crush had inquired about me and wanted to hang out on liberty call. He teased me relentlessly, and I asked him to stop joking about it. He tried to convince me that she wanted to see me the next day. Though I didn't believe him, I went along with it.

The next morning, as we prepared to sign out for the day, my buddy ran up to me and excitedly said, "She's around the corner!" Sure enough, there she was. Hena smiled at me, and we said hello.

I was nervous. We made small talk, and she asked me what I was doing that day. I didn't have any plans and asked if she wanted to hang out. When she said yes, I was thrilled! At that moment, a few guys from her unit walked up and asked her to hang out...in front of me! This made me uncomfortable. I backed up and began to walk away...but she grabbed my hand. Her touch was powerful. She asked where I was going, and I said, "It looks like you have lots of attention. Those guys want to hang out with you."

She said in a sweet voice, "...But I want to hang out with you. Give me a minute to get rid of those guys!" Hena and a girlfriend from her unit, as well as a buddy from my unit and I, rented a limo and took off to savor our freedom. Hena and I spent the entire day together—we went to the ESPN Zone in Chicago. We talked, laughed, and enjoyed ourselves. We bought tee shirts to exchange at the end of the day and wrote personal notes on them. People may think this is crazy, but we also included our social security numbers so we'd know how to find each other! We agreed not to read the notes on the tee shirts until we got back to our barracks. Looking back, the highlight of the day was the moment we first kissed. To date as I write this, that was *the best* kiss of my life!

Hena and I exchanged information to stay in touch. However, she ended up staying in Great Lakes to attend A school for her specialized training, and I ended up in Pensacola, Florida for mine. We lost contact, and that broke my heart. One day, I hope we'll reconnect so I can know how her life has unfolded.

In hindsight, I walked in to boot camp as a boy. I was a know-it-all and thought the world revolved around Travis Angry. I didn't think anyone had the right to tell me what to do. I didn't trust anyone else to help me survive, let alone thrive. It was hard to surrender to someone else's authority. I eventually realized I had to get with the program. When I started to listen to my superiors, everything started to come together. Being part of a team gave me a sense of hope—a desire to succeed and to be the best. That experience helped me to see the power in letting go of my egotistical needs in order to focus on working and serving others. Those nine weeks of boot camp helped me learn to sustain myself for life. I walked out a strong, teachable man.

> Those nine weeks of boot camp helped me learn to sustain myself for life. I walked out a strong, teachable man.

Moving on to school training was remarkable; I learned how to implement the core values as a Navy sailor. Integrity, honor, and accountability became part of my mission. I made friends and sharpened my job skills. I only stayed two weeks in Pensacola, and then was transferred across the country to Lemoore Naval Station in California. While there, I learned the ins and out of my new occupation as a "brown shirt." This is the rank used to describe Plane Captains on aircraft carriers. The "brown shirts" are the individuals who maintain pilots' aircraft. Comparative to maintaining an SUV, my job was to wash, fuel, and make sure everything was in working order for the person who would operate the airplane. I enjoyed seeing the Navy pilots train and take off. I even affectionately called the F-18 Hornet Jet assigned to me "my baby." After all the hard work and dedication that went into my job, I considered it a joy and an honor to watch her fly.

When I received my permanent orders that said I was heading to Atsugi, Japan Naval Air Facility, I wasn't too thrilled. I was headed to the other side of the world. I was scared because I was leaving my family and traveling so far away. Eventually, I had to accept it and change my point of view—which I did. The orders took me to a Fighter Squadron, FA-192 Golden Dragons. My commercial flight flew northwest towards Seattle and crossed over Alaska and east towards Japan. Seeing the world below was amazing. As we landed in Japan, I was like a little kid, all smiles, and I reported to my new home—Atsugi Naval Air Facility.

I settled into my new room, lucky enough not to have a roommate, and reported to my new unit. I then met the man who would have an influential effect on me and hold a special place in my heart. His name was Master Chief Petty Officer (MCP) Polk.

Polk was tough. He was a thick-muscled, light-skinned, black man. When he walked into a room, he demanded respect and received it. He was a no-nonsense master chief; his walk was arrogant, and his talk was precise and direct. He wasn't politically correct; instead, he went "by the book." I had a lot of respect for him. I watched his every move and how he portrayed himself around the sailors in our unit. He led by example and loved physical training. I had to go to his office many times, and I hated it. I challenged the authority of my master chief on the direction of my naval career, and looking back, I learned a valuable lesson—to respect my chain of command.

I still remember my first deployment. It was May 2002, and our ship was the USS Kitty Hawk. At the time, it was not decommissioned but was considered the oldest aircraft carrier in the fleet. When I first reported for deployment, I was extremely nervous while standing at parade rest in "manning the rails." This is when all sailors line up on the deck of the ship, facing outward—a kind of salute and Navy tradition that signifies when a ship sets sail or returns from sea. The USS

Kitty Hawk was to set sail the next morning. That afternoon, everyone reported to the flight deck. I was blown away when I saw four F-18 fighter jets shoot across the skies. It was amazing to see them land. This went on for hours until all of the aircraft were secure.

AN Travis D. Angry

Now, I felt as if I were a true sailor. I was a big fan of aircraft, and I loved this experience. The only challenge I faced was the sleeping quarters. They were tight and didn't accommodate my height comfortably. My schedule—twelve hours dedicated to sleeping and twelve hours spent working— was a challenge, but I made it work. The scariest part was my first night learning the ropes as a plane captain. I had to shadow a shipmate who liked to make jokes and play pranks. It happened to be my night to get "punked." He took me on the flight deck when it was pitch dark and told me to stand behind the jet blast barrier. He said he'd be right back, so I just stood there, chains on my shoulders, as I waited. Next thing I knew, I heard the throttle of an F-16 Tomcat and dropped to the ground because the penetration from the heat and blast were unbearable! It reminded me of the movie "Top Gun"…my shipmate definitely took me to the "danger zone!" Everyone started laughing…except me. I was pissed! I thought I was going to die! Obviously, I didn't; and even though I was scared nearly to death, that experience toughened me up even more. I learned a lot and started to do my job very well. I loved what I did and enjoyed the interaction with the pilots. My job was to make sure their planes were ready to go so they could take off without any issues.

The best experience of this deployment was our first port call. I didn't know what a port call was until we arrived in Singapore. It was an amazingly beautiful country, and we were there for four days. All sailors were assigned ship duty—mine was for the second day. Though the tasks could be grueling, I welcomed the break and enjoyed sightseeing and learning about the country.

My attitude since the beginning of deployment had changed. I now loved deployment, and port calls made it worth every moment on the ship. We set sail again, and off we went to navigate the blue seas. Training began again, leading me to become an experienced plane captain. Often, because I enjoyed it so much, I found myself on the flight deck more often, even during my time off work. I watched the sun rise and set from the deck many times. I appreciated those quiet moments—thinking about life and admiring God's creation.

As deployment came to an end, liberty call and the sweet taste of temporary freedom was on the horizon. I was getting homesick and started to plan a trip to Miami.

When I finally arrived, my mother wouldn't stop doting over me. She even paraded me around in my uniform to all her girlfriends and their daughters! My dad also played matchmaker—trying to get me to the church and hitched as fast as God would allow! As kooky and fun as our visit was, this vacation ended early. I received a phone call from my unit saying I needed to return to Japan and prepare for deployment to Iraq. I hopped on a plane and reported back to my unit. Immediately, I had to get ready to deploy. I grabbed my sea bag and gear, loaded the bus, and reported as ordered. I kept thinking: *I'm actually going to war!* My heart pumped quickly, and I wondered if I'd ever see my family again. We set sail and started training immediately.

As we sailed from Yokosuka into the Indian Ocean, our expedition allowed us to witness the most incredible views. When the sun hit the edge of darkness, the skies lit up into the most glorious glow! We trained all the way to the Persian Gulf. In order for the fighter jets to avoid radar detection, we performed night operations. Watching an F-14 Tomcat build up its turbo blast and watching fire shoot out of the engines during takeoff were both exhilarating and provided such an adrenaline rush...I loved every moment! During this voyage, all sailors aboard the ship prepared the USS Kitty Hawk to navigate through *the most dangerous spot on Earth*: the Straits of Hormuz. This passage was known to be a very tight squeeze—only allowing ships to enter one by one, right after each other. This scene took me back to boot camp—where we'd go through different maneuvers, learn different battle stations, and man our posts with loaded arms. The Kitty Hawk Battle Group included several ships, a tanker-refuel ship, and a submarine, altogether holding about five thousand Navy sailors and Marines. Now, here we were, uncertain what would come next—but the crew was battleship ready.

Once we navigated through the Straits of Hormuz, all was safe, and we proceeded to the Persian Gulf. While there, we conducted flight operations into Iraq. The fighter jets took off from the airstrip of the ship. Word came back that we had lost a jet from my unit. The pilot was married and a father to two kids. He was our first loss. Reality set in: We were sitting in a war zone. *Travis, you are in a war. You are not safe.* This really hit home when I witnessed the burial at sea. We were in the hangar bay on the ship. Thousands of Navy sailors and Marines were lined up by unit, standing in formation to honor this fallen comrade. I thought about his kids growing up without a dad, and I was deeply grateful that my father was still alive. I was extremely sad as I thought about my life, but it put everything into perspective. This situation made me realize the value of our country...and of service. I also thought about those who had already paid the ultimate sacrifice—their courage and what the uniform really meant. That's when I fell deeply in love with the US military.

One of the most joyous moments during my deployment came when Fox News interviewed some of the sailors on the ship. I was one of the chosen. I said, "Hi, my name is Airman Travis Angry. I'm serving on the Kitty Hawk in the Persian Gulf. I want to say hi to my mom and dad. I love you, and I'll be home soon!" A couple of weeks later, I called my dad and found out he had seen me on the news!

In the middle of this deployment, sitting in the Persian Gulf, someone said we'd experience a desert storm. I highly doubted it, because we were in the middle of the sea! That afternoon, all doors to the outside were closed. Within a few hours, the flight deck was open, and what I saw next blew my mind. Dust coated our flight deck as well as our planes! It was a sight I had never witnessed. This sucked for me, because as a plane captain, I had to clean the jets…which took forever. I, along with many other plane captains, went straight to work.

At this point, I was pumped, focused, and ready to go. Training went out the window—the "real deal" was upon us. We received orders for our mission to begin on March 19, 2003. Aircraft were prepared, Hornet and Tomcat jets were headed for Iraq, and missiles were launched. Not long after witnessing the night sky light up with activity, I looked at the TV and saw President Bush address the nation. I was a focused plane captain. I wanted my pilot to be fully taken care of. My success meant that he had a good chance of returning safely, and I took my job seriously. My country's citizens were depending on us, and I did *not* want to let them down.

As if that desire needed to be tested, I happened to get hurt one night while on the flight deck. I did not have my flashlight with me, and when I tried to find the staircase leading to the lower deck, I fell about ten feet and was knocked unconscious! Fortunately, some sailors found me, because the next thing I knew, I was lifted onto a stretcher and taken to the hospital compartment of the ship. I was in serious pain! The doctor informed me that I had sustained minor injury to my spinal cord, and to consider myself lucky. God really blessed me that night by protecting me from worse injury. The injury kept me in bed for days until I was cleared to return to duty.

As my deployment came to an end and the USS Kitty Hawk began heading back to Japan, I took time to reflect upon different aspects of my life. I called these "reflection moments," or times in which I found myself looking at the value of life. I thanked God for bringing my shipmates and me home safely. I didn't know it at the time, but this first deployment would not be my last.

One of the lessons I learned when I came home from this first deployment was how countries relate to one another. This point was driven home during the time I was manning the rails as the ship arrived into port in Yokosuka, Japan. As I stood on the deck, I looked across and saw the Japanese sailors on their ships manning the rails to welcome us home. This was a powerful and emotional experience. I learned firsthand what it means to represent my country in a time of war. I learned about respect between nations.

I would continue to go on many operations, including a winter deployment to Korea. Being a plane captain when the weather conditions were horrible was tough. I had a bad attitude, and my productivity was low. This took a lot out of me, but still, it made me stronger. That is what I loved about the military: It made me much stronger than when I first started. Boot camp broke me down, and the Navy built me into a man of fortitude.

As my two year Navy career came to a close, I was done and felt complete. It was time to return home. Even though I didn't end my Navy career as I anticipated, I was thankful for what I had learned and how well prepared I was for the next phase of my life.

As I was discharged from the Navy in August of 2003, I noticed a large mass under my left armpit. I went to the clinic on base in Japan to see the severity of what happened. The doctors told me they weren't concerned about it and not to worry. I followed their advice and finished processing out of the military at the San Diego Naval Base. I went to the hospital there to have my final

> As I was discharged from the Navy in August of 2003, I noticed a large mass under my left armpit.

medical screening and asked for a second opinion. The diagnosis was the same as the first: There was nothing to worry about. I headed home to Miami, and because I was no longer on active duty, I had to check into the VA hospital there. Being surrounded by veterans who served in previous wars made me miss the Navy. My transition as a veteran back to civilian life proved extremely difficult. As I was checked out by doctors at the VA hospital, the same prognosis was given—nothing's wrong. The mass under my left armpit seemed to have grown, however, and I wasn't satisfied with the VA hospital's answers. In September 2003, I decided to try another local hospital—Memorial Hospital West, in Pembroke Pines—for another opinion. The test results came back negative, so, against my better judgment, I let it go.

I would like to honor and pay tribute to all of our fallen soldiers,
marines, sailors, airmen, coast guardsmen, veterans past and present.
Thank you for your service. You make all the difference in the world.
I respect you.
God bless you, each and every day.

CHAPTER 4

HEALTH

*"Courage is not the absence of fear. It's the
ability to go forward in spite of your fear."*
—Pastor Don Wilson

Both of my parents were thrilled to have me home. My mom made my favorite meals, and Dad and I swapped stories about our involvement with the military. It didn't take long for me to discover that I needed to find my identity as a citizen again. As a veteran, I realized I needed some type of direction. I didn't know what to do, where to go, or where to start. No VA programs that I was aware of existed to help with this transition…it was all up to me. Before I knew it, a month had passed, and I found myself living in the "efficiency room" at my parents' home. Though my father and I had our ups and downs, our relationship remained fair. Dad asked me what my next move was going to be. My brothers were out living their lives and doing their own thing—my dad wanted me to do the same. During this uncertainty, my mother and I grew closer. Though she was studying to get her master's degree in education, she was still very concerned about me. My mother was my rock and offered advice and a listening ear anytime I needed it. As I wrestled with my unforeseen plans, I had a conversation with my neighbor, who also was like a mother figure to me. She inquired about the Navy and my plans now that I was home. I opened up to her about my struggles in figuring out those plans. I also told her about how I had attended Chapel while serving in the Navy, and how it had been a comfort. We talked about me getting myself plugged into a church in Miami, and she suggested I attend Flamingo Baptist.

This church helped me to see the difference in Christianity—as a relationship rather than a religion. Flamingo helped me understand the Bible in a way I never understood as a child. As a youngster, I attended Church of God of Prophecy with my parents. It was the thing to do. This was more of a Southern-style, Pentecostal church. When I attended family functions, I didn't understand why we held hands, prayed, kneeled, and worshipped. I was a youngster with a short attention span, and I often resisted participating. However, when I went to Flamingo, my experience in knowing what it meant to be a Christian changed. I attended a small group Bible study. I was surrounded by people who practiced "religion" in a much more loving way. Attending this church gave me the opportunity to do volunteer work in my community—I served others in a way that differed from my service in the military. This experience was very significant to my growth as a person and as a Christian. I finally started to get into a groove with the church, and I was happy.

"Travis, what happened to you? You lost so much weight!" my friend Nick asked as we stood outside my parents' garage together and shook hands. It was the summer of 2004, and I had been home from the Navy for about a year. It had been almost two years since Nick had seen me; I told him I felt fine, and I didn't think any more of it. We hung out that night and had dinner at the Hard Rock Café in Hollywood, Florida.

It was September 2004, and I went to the Miami VA for a routine visit to check on my back. I wanted to make sure the injuries I had sustained in Iraq had not worsened. The nurse drew some blood and asked me to wait. About fifteen minutes went by, and a physician told me to go upstairs to the hematology/oncology department. I had no idea what was happening; I was clueless, especially when it came to the medical terminology he used.

I went upstairs and met with Dr. Carlos Robles in the hematology/oncology department. He looked at my blood work and said the words I will never forget: "I *think* this may be Hodgkin's disease."

"What is that?" I asked quizzically and with a concerned tone.

When the doctor told me it was a form of cancer, my heart sunk! I started in with questions: "What?! Doc, is this a mistake? Why do I feel fine? I don't feel sick, so how can this be?" I had so many questions, but he wasn't 100 percent certain. Dr. Robles said that further tests would need to be conducted. He then sent me to another area of the hospital to get x-rays.

I had to wait for the results, so I went home and told my parents. When they saw the grievous look on my face, theirs reflected back to me. My parents told me they'd pray for me. I was so confused. I couldn't fathom what was about to happen to me. I didn't feel sick; I *actually* felt strong.

Within a day or two of the finding, I met my team of doctors and nurses. They took me through the diagnostic process and ran more tests, including more blood work. Dr. Robles told me I needed a biopsy on the grapefruit-sized mass to determine if it was for sure cancer. They set up the surgery, and when the surgeon told me he wanted me awake during the procedure, I said, "No way! Put me to sleep, I don't want to see it!" It was October 25, 2004, when the doctors rolled me into the operating room. I saw the surgeon put on his gloves, and before I knew it, the oxygen had put me to sleep. I wore my headphones and listened to music during the procedure to help me relax. I had chosen a special song by the Christian group, Mercy Me, titled, "I Can Only Imagine." I lied there with the song on repeat. As I listened to every word, I started to pray and ask God for direction in this situation. My body was now in His hands. When I awoke in the recovery room, I felt alright. Nurse Sandra made sure I was okay, and the doctor told me the surgery went well.

A few weeks later, I went to the VA and visited the oncology department again. The mass on my left armpit was still the size of a grapefruit. Dr. Robles called for more tests: blood work and a bone marrow biopsy from my spine without anesthesia. He wanted to determine how far the disease had spread. It was an outpatient procedure—the doctor sterilized the area of my sternum and then injected a small needle filled with lidocaine to numb the injection site. The syringe was then used to draw out the necessary amount of bone marrow the doctor needed to test. The procedure lasted about a half hour and was both painful and draining. I was left feeling helpless and scared.

It became a wait-and-see game. I hated waiting! I wanted to know the condition of my health.

During this time, I was so grateful for my new church. One of the members from Flamingo Baptist often visited me during my appointments at the VA. I received a phone call from one of the men in my small group who offered me a full scholarship to the Promise Keepers Men's Conference in Orlando. I accepted the scholarship, not really knowing what to expect. In retrospect, I knew

It became a wait-and-see game. I hated waiting! I wanted to know the condition of my health.

God was guiding me, because Dr. Robles called after I hung up the phone with my friend and told me he needed to see me in his office right away. I asked why, but he wouldn't tell me; I lost my cool and frantically said, "Doctor, just tell me!"

Dr. Robles was very straightforward and said, "Mr. Angry, *you have* been diagnosed with Hodgkin's disease and I *need* to see you. We can begin treatment tomorrow." The air literally left my lungs. I sat there on the sofa, stunned. It was a surreal moment—as if it were happening to someone else and not to me. I couldn't talk. I must have sat there for two hours without moving—shocked. I thought about my life: *Could it be ending so soon? What were God's plans for me?* I thought about many things.

The reality that this disease could end my life hit me hard. I realized that my faith wasn't as strong as it needed to be. If I was going to beat this illness, then my biggest hope had to be my faith.

The day Dr. Robles told me I had cancer was Thursday, November 4, 2004. It's a day that forever will be etched in my mind. I set a date to begin treatment the following week. A lot of things in life were rapidly changing—however, my plans to attend the Promise Keepers event that weekend did not. On Friday, November 5, 2004, I packed my things for Orlando and headed to Flamingo Baptist to meet with everyone. There to see us off was the man responsible for my scholarship. Unfortunately, I can't remember his name, but he was a senior, probably in his 70s, with lots of gray, curly hair. He had kind eyes and spoke with a lot of wisdom. He, along with the church staff, prayed for our bus ride and our soon-to-be weekend. We arrived in Orlando four hours later, had dinner, and headed over to attend the first night of Promise Keepers. I was very relaxed, and I still did not know what to expect.

We entered Amway Arena, and the place was packed with men and their sons. The event began with great music and fellowship, and all the men seemed to be in tune with their environment. The theme of the event was "Uprising: The Revolution of a Man's Soul." One by one, the speakers came up to address the audience. One of the speakers I remember very well, but only by his last name: White. He had battled leukemia and talked about how his faith was the center of his courage. Mr. White's story resonated with me. It was as if his story paralleled the very news I had received just the day before. He encouraged all of us to get into the game of life and value being a man of honor. Though I surely didn't feel like it, Mr. White's message echoed the truth, saying that God created *me* to be a man of honor. The words of Mr. White's speech made such an impact on my spirit; to this day, I have been able to recall nearly every word.

After Friday's event, on the bus ride to the hotel, I felt pumped spiritually, but physically, grew very weak. My body felt worn down, and I quickly grew tired. I decided to turn in for the night.

I woke up the next morning, ate a good breakfast, and headed back to the Arena with the Flamingo Baptist men to enjoy our last day of Promise Keepers. The most powerful experience of my life to date happened at that conference—even more powerful than the cancer. It was Saturday, November 6, 2004, at nine a.m., and about fifteen thousand men, including me, stood up and started singing, "Amazing Grace." I tried to stay standing, but couldn't because the cancer had made me feel so lethargic and weak. I sat there and cried. "Amazing Grace" was the song that influenced my father's life and helped him find Christ in 1979. Now, here I sat, twenty-five years later, feeling that connection to my earthly father. *"I once was lost, but now I'm found..."* As these fifteen thousand men and I continued to sing, I felt the Holy Spirit enter my heart. These powerful lyrics solidified my connection with God—now, *my* Heavenly Father. It was the most amazing feeling in the world. I felt brand new, and I longed for more.

As I walked to the bus for the ride home, emotionally charged, I thought about what would happen once I arrived back in Miami. The movie, "Gladiator," played on the bus, and as I watched it, I felt that the strength and encouragement I had received from my fellow Promise Keeper attendees, coupled with the challenge Mr. White issued in his speech, had helped to build my focus. I was determined that I would beat this cancer. I looked around the bus and realized that I was amongst some great men—I wanted to be courageous too. I knew life had more in store for me, and I wanted God to be at the center of it all. I made that commitment to Christ and pledged that I would walk this cancer journey with Him. By the time I arrived home, I had changed in the most important way a human being can change: I was determined to leave my old ways behind and stand unwavering in my promise to prosper spiritually.

> I was determined that I would beat this cancer.

> By the time I arrived home, I had changed in the most important way a human being can change: I was determined to leave my old ways behind and stand unwavering in my promise to prosper spiritually.

The night I got home from Orlando, I said my prayers and woke up the next day with a new attitude and new perspective. The day had arrived for me to meet with my doctors and nurses to begin my treatment. I couldn't wait; I actually was getting excited. I caught the bus and then monorail to the VA Hospital. I walked into my doctor's office with a message. I was clear on what I wanted to say, and the first thing that came out of my mouth was, "Doc, we've got some work to do. *I am determined* to beat this cancer, so let's get started."

He smiled, and when I saw the focus and determination in Dr. Robles's eyes, I wanted even more to be known as a cancer survivor. My military weight was an average of 224 pounds, but when I got on the scale, I weighed 147. I had lost so much weight; the cancer was spreading, and the doctor knew it. It was determined that I was at stage two, which meant I was still in the early stages of this disease.

I had an outpatient procedure that required the surgeon to place a port-a-cath in the upper left side of my chest. This catheter-like device connected to a vein under my skin and allowed my doctor to intravenously inject drugs into my port during chemo treatments. This device helped ease some of the pain from getting poked by needles multiple times. During my chemo treatments, I would often sit in this oncology room for hours surrounded by older veterans who had fought in previous wars. Even though I was the youngest person, as I mentioned earlier, I made friends with them. I was bored very easily, but stayed strong and maintained my focus throughout the treatment. At that point, my family was nowhere to be found—my brothers in fact never once came to see me in the hospital.

I couldn't believe it. I sat there, with no support. I began to feel sad, isolated, and heartbroken.

One day, unexpectedly, my father showed up to the hospital. I was shocked. He walked into the room, Bible in hand, looking dapper and with this determined look on his face. One look at me, and I could tell he was truly affected by seeing me go through this ordeal. Dad and I talked for a while, and he placed his Bible on the armrest of my chair. We prayed, we cried, and for the first time, we talked about our differences. He told me what he expected of me in continuing on and overcoming my battle. During that conversation, we reconciled our differences and focused on me getting better. He infused me with hope.

During my next round of chemo, my mother came to visit me. That was difficult because I didn't want my mom to see me so sick. I felt numb. She told me she had informed our family in the Bahamas about my condition, and that everyone was praying for me. She smiled at me. I knew she was trying to be brave. I felt sad when I wanted to feel strong, especially for my mom.

That scenario finally broke me and immediately motivated me to call my good friend, Jennifer Crotty, in Phoenix. I had met Jennifer back in 2000 while working for America West Airlines in Fort Lauderdale. I spent three weeks in Arizona for training at the America West headquarters and during that time, some fellow coworkers and I went to Hooters in Tempe. Jennifer was our waitress. At that time, as I mentioned, I also worked as a manager/producer for my own music company, Set It Off Entertainment. I had asked Jennifer what she did, and she told me she worked and went to school but wished she could be a singer. Jennifer said she sang karaoke; my coworkers encouraged her to sing a few lines for me and convinced her that I was really in the music business. Back then, we ended up working together. She would fly to Miami and I would fly to Arizona. I once put together a photo shoot to promote her and arranged a few gigs for her.

During our talk, Jen suggested that I consider moving to Arizona to get away. I told her that if I moved, I would never live in Florida again. I went home from the hospital and prayed about my decision to move. I thought about my doctor and how we discussed my claim against the VA for my original misdiagnosis—stating that there wasn't anything wrong with me. I knew the funds I received from my claim would help greatly to ease the burden of moving. I also knew it was time to move forward; but I wanted to make sure that if I did this, I would be focused on succeeding and going to a place where I would be happy and enjoy my life. The hard part would be talking to my dad and convincing him that this change was necessary for me to move forward. I decided to put it off for a bit.

I decided that my official move date to Arizona would be on January 5, 2005. I was leaving Florida for good, and nothing was going to change my mind. My family wasn't close at that point anyway, and that didn't help me feel supported day to day. Seeing each other only when someone married or passed away wasn't enough, and in my eyes, didn't constitute a family. I didn't want to be a part of that anymore. I thought it would be more beneficial to set out on my own and start my own family. I couldn't force my family to be close—I wanted to be in a place where I could battle and beat this cancer, and to me, that place was Arizona.

I made my plans. I booked my plane ticket, ordered my car to be shipped, and made medical arrangements with the VA to transfer all my medical records to Phoenix. Then, there was the hard part—going into Dad's office and telling him about the move. I wasn't nervous, but I wasn't looking forward to his response. I said, "Dad, I need to tell you something."

"What?" he asked curiously.

"I made an important decision."

"You're going to finish school?"

I said, "No, I'm moving to Phoenix, Arizona, and I'm not coming back. I'm not coming back because in the past I was known to say things and never follow through." I wanted my dad to understand that this wasn't a vacation.

Once again, he asked, "Why?"

"I'm not happy here. I want to be in a place where I'm happy and I can beat this cancer." After I said that, he got really mad and heated.

He yelled at me and told me how bad of a decision I was making, and that I would be running back home like I usually did. He said he would end up taking care of me for the rest of my life.

I said, "*Dad you've done enough. I need to be a man and go create my own kingdom and start my life and family...like you did.*"

He wasn't trying to hear it and just wanted me to stay.

I said, "Dad you've done enough. I need to be a man and go create my own kingdom and start my life and family...like you did."

I said, "Dad, I am sorry, but here is my plane ticket. *This is serious.*"

He started to cry, and we hugged and prayed. Dad took it *hard.* Things got so bad that I had to go talk to our family friend, Rodney Polite. Rodney was my dad's longtime friend who helped discipline my brothers and me when we were out of control. I went to his house and told Mr. Polite that I needed to get out from under my father's wing. "Why won't Dad accept me leaving? He's been on me for staying home this late in my life."

Mr. Polite looked at me and said, "Travis, if you want to go to Arizona, then go. Your father will be okay. I will talk with him."

A few nights later, my parents and I went to dinner with Mr. Polite. We had a very in-depth, heart-to-heart talk. I could finally leave Florida on good terms, and that was the most important thing to me.

Ready to start the next chapter of my battle, I headed to Fort Lauderdale International Airport for my flight on America West Airlines to Phoenix. Flying over the desert was awesome because it gave me a glimpse into my future, and I loved God's plan for me. Jennifer was waiting for me at the airport. When I landed in Phoenix, she took me to Wal-Mart and loaded my cart with things I needed. We then headed over to my new apartment in the Ahwatukee community in the southern part of Phoenix. I saw the apartment and fell in love. I loved my new furniture. Jennifer had helped bring everything to fruition. I was thankful to be on my own again. To me, Jennifer lived out the true definition of friendship.

I started treatments within days of arriving in Phoenix. After I was processed into the Carl T. Hayden VA Medical Center, it was very important that I stay on track with my treatment. Both Miami and Phoenix VA Hospitals' oncology departments communicated very well on my behalf in making sure that my treatment schedule would not be affected by this move.

When it was time to go to the hospital and check in, I met my new team of doctors and nurses. Thomas Kummet, M.D., was my chief doctor. The senior nurse, Dennis Pebbles, checked me in and did my evaluation. This was how I was welcomed into cancer treatment in my new, home city. Dennis and I had many interactions; he told me I was a fighter and that my positive attitude was apparent and would aid me in my healing.

During that time, and within one month of the move, I was enjoying the city and going to Diamondbacks and Suns sporting events. I entertained myself, but something was missing. I wanted to grow my faith and needed a church community to call home. One of my former pastors from Flamingo Baptist had told me about a church in Phoenix called Christ's Church of the Valley (CCV), and said I should check into it. CCV was way up north, too far to drive, so I tried a church in Mesa that was closer to my apartment. I went to the early service at nine a.m., but I didn't like it at all. As I drove home that Sunday morning, I figured I would just watch the NFL playoffs on TV, but then my thinking changed. I was driving on Highway 60, heading west towards the I-10 interstate, which was taking me home. I had Christian music playing, and I kept thinking about this church, CCV. Should I or should I not go? I was driving in the middle lane and needed to make a quick decision: *Do I go home or drive north?* I immediately got in the right lane and headed north on Interstate I-17 to Happy Valley Road.

I got off at the exit and headed west to CCV, located on the southwest corner of 67 Avenue.

As I looked at the church, it was huge and reminded me of an arena. I drove into the parking lot where people were directing cars. Others smiled at me and introduced themselves. Everyone was very cordial. I walked to the front entrance appearing as if I was lost. Pastor Doug Carter came over and introduced himself. I told him I was new and looking for a home church. Pastor Carter told me more about CCV and then gave me a brief tour. I was impressed with the landscape and how beautiful the grounds were. I thanked him for the tour and found a seat just as the service began. The music started, and I thought it was interesting—not too over the top. As communion was passed out to everyone, I sat there and prayed. The sermon "God's Incredibles," followed suit.

The senior pastor, Dr. Don Wilson, gave a timely message. Just as Mr. White's speech at the Promise Keepers' event resonated with me, in the same way, Pastor Don's words were finding their place in my heart. I wanted to hear more words of wisdom, so I decided to return the following week. His words struck a chord in me again. I was beginning to love this new church. Eventually, I met more pastors, joined the singles ministry, and made new friends.

I enjoyed interacting with the singles ministry every week. No more night clubs or parties; I had found new friends here. As I started to get more involved, I was introduced to Chad Ryan, who was well known around the group. He and I hit it off well. We had lunch and got to know each other. Chad invited me to different socials, and at one point, he asked me to come to a party. He had a friend that he wanted me to meet: Tom Still. He said Tom was in flight school at Luke Air Force Base and was training to fly the F-16 fighter jet. I walked into the party and saw Chad. He introduced me to some of his friends; it was great to meet more people within the group. Chad located Tom and brought us into the backyard. Chad told us both that we needed to talk to each other—that our stories were similar.

Tom and I talked and shared our life stories. I was in shock because we shared so many similarities. We both served in the military and battled the same form of cancer, Hodgkin's Lymphoma. We talked about how it had affected our careers and how we liked the same hobbies—such as basketball and football. Tom and I stood in the backyard for the rest of the night talking and laughing, developing a new friendship.

During my treatment, Dr. Kummet informed me that they needed to conduct more tests. They discovered that I had a blood clot located in my right arm, and it was serious. I had only been living in Arizona for one month; I didn't know anybody all that well. I had no family nearby, and now my doctor was informing me that I had to be admitted to the hospital for an overnight stay for monitoring. Though I stayed a few nights to get the blood clot under control, I was so distressed and lonely that I didn't know what was happening. I had great doctors and nurses who took care of me and helped me to get through it. The senior nurse, Dennis Pebbles, used his witty humor to cheer me up. However, being in a new city and not having any support system or family members nearby was very tough on me. My parents were very worried and prayed constantly. I was very scared about losing my life.

One day, out of the blue, Chad Ryan and Tom Still visited me at the hospital. The care of this church truly touched my heart. I was eventually released from the hospital, and I headed home. My aftercare routine required me to give myself shots for the blood clots, but I was too scared. Thankfully, my friend Jennifer stepped in and helped me handle them.

I went to chemotherapy every two weeks, four to five hours a day, often just sitting there. I sat back and reflected on my life. As I stated in the introduction to this book, which I will repeat here because it is so crucial to the theme of this book: "I marveled at the extreme highs and lows: my troubled teenage years, dropping out of high school, my military experience, my relationship with my family. Throughout every incident, there seemed to be one recurring theme: *change*. I'm just an ordinary man who's had some difficult times, but no matter what happened to me, I always possessed the ability to better my circumstances. Struck with an epiphany, I asked the nurse on duty for a pen and paper and jotted down the most important phrase I'd ever written: **CHANGE: If I Can, You Can."**

> If I could go from the battlefield of Iraq to a hospital bed in the VA Hospital in Phoenix and come out on top, others, too, could be capable of creating something positive amidst change. To me, positive change started with believing and leaning on faith for understanding.

We all have to face challenges and hardships. If I could go from the battlefield of Iraq to a hospital bed in the VA Hospital in Phoenix and come out on top, others, too, could be capable of creating something positive amidst change. To me, positive change started with believing and leaning on faith for understanding. I chose to lean on God and believe He would provide direction for my life. If God wanted to use my story as an example to overcome, so be it.

I worked through the tough days of treatment. Often, this was very hard, because I drove myself to the hospital, and some days I was very weak. Having drugs pumped into you for four to five hours at a time is difficult; but thankfully, the military had made me tough mentally, and I managed.

One day, I walked into an appointment, and Dr. Kummet had a smile on his face. He told me I was done with

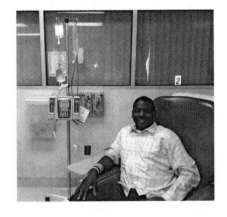

chemotherapy. I was excited, but he said that the treatment wasn't complete, and that he was sending me to an outside center for radiation treatment in West Phoenix. I engaged in radiation at West Valley Radiology in Goodyear, Arizona, for one and a half months. The process was fairly simple. I went every two weeks, and didn't have any complications from the treatment. I would lie on my back on the exam table so they could position me just right and radiate the areas that needed it. Radiation treatment lasted approximately thirty to forty minutes each visit. After it was all said and done, I went back to the VA see Dr. Kummet as well as his colleague, Dr. Salvatore.

That day, I didn't know it, but I was about to get some of the biggest news of my life to date—if not the biggest. As I was waiting for the appointment, my cell phone rang. It was the CCV singles ministry pastor, Chad Goucher. He wanted to pray with me before my appointment began. We talked, and he prayed. I was overjoyed by the phone call, because it helped to settle my nerves.

> That day, I didn't know it, but I was about to get some of the biggest news of my life to date—if not the biggest.

I then walked into Dr. Kummet's office and had my vitals taken. I had my weight and height checked, a nurse took my blood, and Dr. Kummet looked at everything from my CAT and PET scans to my medical records and said the beautiful words all cancer patients hope to hear: "Your cancer, Mr. Angry, is officially in remission."

I almost cried, but couldn't because I was jumping up and down! Tuesday, June 7, 2005, was a day of glory; it was the day I became cancer free! I had survived the cancer that had once plagued my entire body! The cancer was no longer there. To God be the glory!

I called my parents and gave them the news. They were thankful to God. Everyone was relieved! I shared the news with my new best friend, Tom Still, and began my annual tradition of treating myself to a five star dinner, which I still do to this day. (Every year, I go to my favorite restaurant, Sapporo, in Scottsdale, on the anniversary of my "cancer free" announcement. I love to celebrate this victory in my life!)

My health had been restored to me, and I believe that was greatly in part because of Dr. Kummet's and Dr. Salvatore's knowledge of my disease. They educated me on the effects of Stage IIB Hodgkin's Lymphoma, and how this form of cancer could become aggressive and rampant. Though 100 percent recovery rate couldn't be guaranteed, my doctors had been optimistic that, as I had worked to live a healthy lifestyle—eating right, exercising regularly, and following a positive regimen—I'd achieve better results...and it had worked!

Now that I was physically doing better, I wanted to do something special to commemorate, so I decided to join CCV. I attended "Class 100" —the church's orientation for new members. Pastor Don led the class, and I loved everything he said about CCV and how he presented himself. I thought his messages were on point, and I enjoyed his leadership. It looked like I had found a mentor. After I joined the church, I decided to get baptized. I asked Tom to be baptized with me. He agreed. I was cancer free, and this was my way of celebrating. Pastor Peter Strubhar, Tom, and I all got into the water and affirmed a belief in Christ. When I was dunked in that water, I died to self, and when I rose, I felt renewed and energized.

> From that moment, I recognized that my outlook on life was changing and my faith was growing. I still had more work to do in becoming a man of honor, but knew I was headed in the right direction.

From that moment, I recognized that my outlook on life was changing and my faith was growing. I still had more work to do in becoming a man of honor, but knew I was headed in the right direction. I was walking this path to righteousness, and it felt good knowing God was with me every step of the way.

CHAPTER 5

FAMILY

"As you begin changing your thinking, start immediately to change your behavior. Begin to act the part of the person you would like to become. Take action on your behavior. Too many people want to feel, then take action. This never works."

—John C. Maxwell

Becoming a man of honor was still my primary goal. I was thirty years old; I had established a home in Arizona, formed a spiritual foundation, and was involved in a church I really enjoyed. Though I was plugged into a singles ministry and had great friends, I still felt something was missing—I realized that I wanted a family of my own. I decided to try online dating and joined Match.com. This online community had its users fill out a profile showcasing their interests, hobbies, goals, and qualities. While logged onto the website, matches were displayed on the screen based on shared interests and criteria. That's when I saw her—the face of this beautiful woman staring back at me on the computer screen. Her name was Melody. I couldn't stop looking at her picture. As I stared at her photo, I thought about how

I longed for a family built upon a strong spiritual foundation—God's principles and not my own. I desired to have a marriage like my parents had modeled for me. This is how I envisioned my life—just by that one simple glimpse of Melody's photo. Call it what you want: serendipitous, kismet, fate; maybe it was love at first sight...even though I had not yet met Melody in person.

Though the website said we were a match, I doubted that I'd have a shot with her. I took my chances anyway and contacted her. Surprisingly, a few days later, she emailed back! We made "small talk" through our email exchanges, and then one night in August of 2006, I finally got the courage to call her on the phone. Melody lived with her parents in Leavenworth, Washington, and I was in Phoenix, Arizona. Our phone conversation started at 10 p.m. and lasted until 6 a.m. Melody's and my connection was instant. I was in tune with what she shared. We talked about everything—including family, church, relationships, and her daughter, Tatiyana.

I remember sitting on the other end of the phone call, telling myself, "*This is the one.*"

I loved her voice; I could hear her sweet smile through the phone. In my mind's eye, I could envision her long, flowing, brunette hair, encircled by a bright glow. Melody was the equivalent of my high school dream girl come true! We laughed, bonded, and made each other feel special. She talked about her daughter, Tatiyana's, father, and how he wasn't an involved parent. Melody shared that Tatiyana's biological father decided before she was born that he did not want anything to do with her. He chose to not be a part of her life and didn't show up for her birth. Since he never married Melody or stayed in her life, so she was on her own. I thought about our first email exchanges and how Melody had shared photos of Tatiyana. *"How could a man just walk away from this beautiful, little girl?"*

As we talked, Melody surprised me and asked me a very important question: "Could you love my daughter as if she were your own?"

Caught off guard, I paused for a moment and thought about my parents and the values they had instilled in me. Without any doubt and with affirmation, I replied, "Yes, I could." Melody began to cry. There was a bond forming between us. I had touched her heart. Melody knew she had found someone who would love Tatiyana and her both.

From that point on, we talked and text messaged each other every day. Our conversations were about anything and everything, and often contained sweet little sayings that made the other smile. More importantly, Melody and I talked about how our intention wasn't to "date just to date." Though all of this was still fairly new, we believed in our hearts that we wanted to be married, and our conversations reflected that. We talked about our faith, our relationships with our families, and what a future family would look like. Within a few days of discussing these things in depth, Melody became my girl. I was happy and excited not only because Melody was attractive, but because she was as into me as I was into her. Our phone conversations made me feel like we'd known each other forever—but we hadn't...I wanted to meet her! I asked Melody to visit me in Arizona so we could spend time growing our relationship. She said yes to my request.

Before Melody planned her trip, I "met" her parents by telephone so I could introduce myself. Her mom, Judy, was such a gracious woman: kind and sweet just like my mother. A bit later, I talked with her dad, Tim. Though most men would be intimidated, I wasn't nervous; I believed I was a good man and had a lot to offer his daughter. I was anxious to say hello; Melody sweetly gave me some tips: to be myself, to be honest, and to speak from my heart. I did just that. Tim asked me the tough questions like any father would ask: What are your intentions? Are you a Christian? Explain your faith to me. What are your career goals, and do you have a job now? I answered all of his questions with honesty. I felt satisfied about our conversation and looked forward to meeting him. My feelings for Melody had developed rapidly; I was falling in love with her, and my conversation with her parents just solidified that even more.

Our "relationship" might have seemed unorthodox to some, but we were following our hearts. Melody and I continued to talk on the phone, email, and text during the few weeks prior to her visit. Many nights, I'd lie awake, thinking about my future with Melody. I didn't take marriage lightly and planned to stay committed for life—through ups and downs, good times and bad. Melody was the one I wanted to be with; I knew I was going to ask her to marry me, but I didn't know when. Those late night ponderings sent me on a mission. I went to the Arizona Mills Mall to shop for an engagement ring. When I walked into Crescent Jewelers, I saw it—the ring! This was the ring I was going to propose to Melody with! It was a beautiful, white gold wedding set with a princess cut diamond in the center and two smaller diamonds on the side. These precious stones in the engagement setting represented "past, present, and future." Just like those diamonds, that is how I desired life to be with Melody—shining, valuable, and priceless. Right after I picked out the ring, I called Melody's dad, Tim, and told him my intention. I wanted to marry his daughter and asked for his blessing. Tim gave me the green light. I was feeling great about this and wanted to make sure I planned the perfect proposal.

As I thought about her, one thing was for sure: Melody was the only woman who ever gave me the time of day. In the past, I had been rejected—by woman after woman; but now, here was this angel, falling for *me*. I wasn't used to this; having a woman tell me that I was *enough* boggled my mind. I finally had a woman totally into me, and I wasn't going to let her get away. I wanted to take care of Melody for the rest of our lives. I wanted to show her how happy and proud I was to call her my girl.

The weeks went by slowly; but *finally*, August 25 arrived—the time came for Melody to visit Arizona. That same day, a terrorist attack happened in England, and all US airports were on high alert. There was frustration and concern; all flights were cancelled or re-routed. Eventually, Melody made it to Arizona at around eleven p.m.

When Melody walked out of the terminal on that Friday evening and I saw her for the first time, my heart stopped. Everything about her made my insides turn to mush and I had a big, goofy grin on my face. Because Melody had been traveling all day, she was feeling self-conscious about her appearance. However, to me, I saw her natural beauty. When we got to the car, I gave her a little gift to let her know I was thinking of her. It was from Bath and Body Works. She flashed me one of her pretty smiles confirming that she liked her gift.

Our visit started out magnificently. I was elated and wanted to make the weekend one that would be unforgettable. Melody stayed over at my house and slept in the guest room. I woke up to a knock on my door the next morning, and when I opened the door, my mouth dropped open. On the other side of the threshold stood Melody, this beautiful, Caucasian queen. She was already dressed for the day—she donned a simple but cute ensemble, her dark hair lay fanned out over her shoulders, and her emerald eyes twinkled when she smiled at me.

"Good morning! I made you breakfast, Travis."

"Oh really?" I asked in a soft, sleepily voice, feeling self-conscious about the bed-headed look I was sporting.

"Yes. Why don't you go freshen up and then come out to the kitchen," Melody said sweetly.

I hurried and freshened up. When I walked into the kitchen, I saw the breakfast sitting on the kitchen table. Melody had lovingly decorated and arranged waffles, sausage, and fresh fruit on the plate. She was busily doing something in the kitchen, but I took one look at her, and then focused my eyes back on my plate. I picked up my phone and called my dad.

"What's up, Son? How are you doing?" Dad asked when he answered the phone.

"Dad, I found her. Call me crazy; call me what you want, but I found her: my future wife." As Dad and I shared a chuckle, I looked over at Melody, and she flashed me her gorgeous smile.

I hung up with my dad and sat down to enjoy breakfast. Besides my mom, Melody was the first woman to speak my love language—food! Any woman willing to express her love through cooking was a keeper, in my book! Our conversation flowed freely. There were moments we didn't say much because we were too busy blushing and making googly-eyes at one another.

That afternoon, I took Melody to a preseason Cardinals football game against the Pittsburgh Steelers. I looked around the stadium and thought about the next few days. When was I going to propose to Melody? We shared nachos and enjoyed the game; it felt so easy to be around her. Later that afternoon, we went to the 4:30 p.m. service at CCV. Melody looked around and had the same reaction I had about the church—it was big! She liked Pastor Don's message at CCV as well as the music. However, because Melody's dad, Tim, was a pastor of a smaller church back in Leavenworth, she enjoyed that comfort and familiarity on a smaller scale.

After Melody and I ate at CCV's café, we hopped in my black Mazda 6 and headed west to California to visit Melody's sister, Jennifer. She opened up her home and heart. Jennifer was gracious and made me feel comfortable. We ate breakfast at Jennifer's house, and then Melody and I headed to Disneyland. I was excited and nervous at the same time. I knew I wanted to pop the question, but wanted to wait for the right moment. We walked down Disneyland's Main Street and took pictures. Melody wanted to ride on Splash Mountain; I was hesitant, but away we went. I told Melody I didn't like roller coasters; I had felt that way since I was a little kid. Something about the adrenaline rush and feeling out of control while going in a downward motion didn't sit well with me.

Melody's mission was to teach me not to fear the roller coaster. I tried to change the subject, "If I was to ask you to marry me, do I still have to go on Splash Mountain?" I said in front of the crowd waiting to get on the ride.

Caught off guard, Melody looked and me and said, "Yes, you do!"

"No! I'm not going!" I told her playfully. I wasn't going to budge.

Melody decided she still wanted to go on the ride, so she did. People in the crowd smiled at us. We walked over to explore Cinderella's castle. I thought about maybe proposing there, but felt it was overrated because everyone tended to choose that spot. After a few other rides, Melody and I walked over to the Haunted Mansion attraction. While we were in line, I thought about popping the question. Even though it seemed out of the norm for most people, I kept thinking this was the right spot.

Right before we entered the Haunted Mansion, I got down on one knee and asked Melody to marry me. It was a spontaneous moment, and Melody was shocked. She kept asking over and over, "Are you serious? Are you serious?"

I told her I was being serious, and then she said yes!

Wow, was I ecstatic! My dream girl had said yes, and I felt like a new man! I was so delighted; I called my father and told him the good news. My dad's response wasn't what I had hoped though; he thought something was wrong with my state of mind. However, his reaction didn't deter my happiness. Even though I had been rejected by women all my life, God had finally brought someone into my life who loved and wanted to marry me. This was the best feeling in the world, and I wasn't going to let anyone steal my joy.

Melody and I had a fabulous time in California, and as we drove back to Arizona, we talked and planned our lives together. We both agreed that she would move to Arizona. We also talked about me planning a trip to Leavenworth to meet her parents and the rest of her family. Even though I had already received his consent, I wanted to properly ask Melody's dad for his daughter's hand in marriage.

It was our last night together before Melody had to leave Arizona. She got emotional and I reassured her that I was there for her and would see her soon. I told her I loved her and that I was serious about our future together. I drove Melody to Sky Harbor the next day and saw her off. Even though I didn't want her to go, I knew I would see her soon.

The next two weeks flew by quickly. When I arrived in Washington on September 15, 2006, I felt ecstatic. I missed my girl and couldn't wait to see her! I went to the baggage claim to retrieve my luggage. There was my beautiful Melody, holding her one-year-old daughter, Tatiyana, in her arms. Tatiyana and I looked at each other for a good, awkward moment before she gave me a smile. I couldn't take my eyes off of that beautiful, little girl. Inside, I felt excited for the future. My desire—a family of my own—was coming to fruition.

We drove two hours up into the mountains of Leavenworth, Washington. The scenery was breathtaking; I couldn't believe how big the mountains were, and it was awesome to see God's handiwork. When Melody and I arrived at her parents' house, preparations were being made to host a big, family dinner. Melody and I, along with her parents, made a quick stop at the local Safeway supermarket. Tim and I walked into the produce aisle, and it was there that I proclaimed my love for his daughter. I assured Tim that it was my desire to honor Melody, cherish her, care for her, and that she was in good hands. Though I had asked on the phone, I reiterated to Tim in person that it was my desire to ask for Melody's hand. Tim got misty-eyed and gave me his blessing.

When we got back to the house, I met Melody's brother, Danny. He was cool as ice—a great guy. Tim, Melody's dad, introduced me to the extended family. I was shocked when Tim asked me to say a few words. I wasn't prepared; however, I wasn't shy about talking to people either. I told Melody's family a little bit about myself and assured them I had nothing but the best intentions: I was there to claim Melody as my new wife and her beautiful daughter, Tatiyana, as my own. I would be bringing them to Phoenix to start our new life together as a family.

The rest of our visit was pleasant. We went sightseeing and even attended Melody's family church. I met some of the members, and they welcomed me warmly. Listening to Tim's preaching was different from my experience with my own father, but nonetheless, encouraging. He was a man who knew the Word of God and expressed it in a way

I understood. It was reassuring to know that Melody and I shared a similar, godly foundation.

Before we knew it, our trip came to an end. We were ready to head to Phoenix and begin our lives together. Melody's parents took us to lunch and then drove us to the airport in Leavenworth. I focused on taking care of the luggage and checking us in while Melody spent a few, quality moments with her folks to say goodbye. I knew it was very difficult and emotional for Melody, and I did my best to console her. Tim and Judy hugged Melody, Tatiyana, and me—and reiterated their support for us. It was a compassionate moment, and I was thankful for their encouragement. We said goodbye and headed home to Arizona.

In August of 2006, I made two of the biggest decisions of my life. The first was to join the Arizona Army National Guard. The second decision was to marry my girlfriend, Melody Grace Heath. Melody and I had decided to elope. (Because of my dad's upbringing in the oppressive South during the Civil Rights movement, he wasn't fond of interracial relationships. The wound wasn't healed completely, so we thought it best to avoid a scene. Melody's parents were supportive of our wishes). So, on Thursday, September 28, 2006, at one o'clock in the afternoon, Melody and I said, "I do." It was a simple ceremony, and we didn't have a honeymoon. Overall, everything was short, sweet, and to the point.

Before Melody visited me in Arizona for the first time, I had been sworn in as an E-2 Private. I labored under the direction of the chief warrant officer for the Arizona National Guard, John Vitt. Vitt was five feet, 220 pounds, and had curly, black hair. He had a love for ASU and Cardinals' football. He had thirty plus years under his belt in Army Service and directed the reconstitution of equipment that accompanied the 1,400 soldiers deploying/redeploying from a war zone, namely Iraq and Afghanistan. "Chief," as I called Vitt, also supervised numerous civilian contractors that helped ready soldiers of the Arizona Army National Guard.

"Angry, we have to make sure that the techs and the contractors get paid. Keeping track of their leave accrual and the equipment is what you can help me with. There are commercial trucks coming to us with deliveries and orders to pick-up equipment every day. You have to help me keep track of them all, please," Vitt would say on any given day.

"You got it, Chief," was my response to everything.

Our phones rang constantly. I would tell the drivers how to find us on our twelve acre lot. Even if it was after hours, "Chief" would tell me to have vendors bring in the load since it would mean one less headache for the next day. I also prepared welcome packets, arranged necessary appointments, and directed mail for those leaving and returning. I didn't need accolades, but I did want to ensure I was being effective at my post. Chief Vitt let me know that my contributions made a difference and played a positive role in bringing our soldiers home safely.

Melody was my dream come true. I had found the most amazing, beautiful, caring, supportive woman. All those years I had struggled to feel love from my family growing up, I now had in Melody as my partner. She brought purpose and love to my life—she was my best friend. We had our fair share of struggles, but we laughed, we joked, and we did all those cute things that couples do. We went to church together and held hands while we worshipped. The affection I lacked and longed for in my earlier years had now been found through my relationship with Melody. I felt seen and heard and loved. I thought I had died and gone to heaven! I didn't even expect the affection, and yet here she was, giving it freely. All my life, I had been searching, running after love, and here it was in human flesh, in the form of my lovely Melody.

We began to get into a routine. I was serving in the Arizona Army National Guard working from 8 a.m. to 5 p.m. during the week and training one weekend a month. Melody was working at US Airways in the reservations department at night, from 5 p.m. to 11 p.m. The evenings were bonding time for me and Tatiyana. I would spend time with her, fix her dinner, read to her, take her to the park, give her a bath, and put her down for the night. Tatiyana became very attached to me, but Melody did not realize it. I was a father figure in Tatiyana's life—everywhere I went, she would go, too. In January 2007, I considered adopting Tatiyana.

During the first two years, Melody and my marriage met some challenges. Melody started to have regrets over being married. I remember about two months into our marriage; Melody was in the kitchen cooking and started to cry.

"I can't believe I did this. I can't believe I married *you*." Melody said regretfully.

"I can't believe I did this. I can't believe I married *you*." Melody said regretfully.

Those words hit the core of my being.

Melody explained that she felt as though she rushed into marriage and didn't think things through. She told me that God was first in her life, then Tatiyana, her family... *and then me.*

It was a blow that hurt me deeply. Her parents tried to talk to her and offer her counsel, but it didn't help. We were arguing and disagreeing. First, I shut down and tried to avoid confrontation. I was lured into the back and forth because I began to see that Melody was a very dominant woman. Eventually, I realized that she was in driver's seat, and I thought I needed to overpower her with my manhood—meaning I would raise my voice, yell, and scream to be heard. We were a mess. How could I salvage this?

Though we would argue constantly, Melody wanted to stop working and be a stay-at-home mom. I understood her desire, but I felt she needed to work and help support Tatiyana. We weren't agreeing on the direction of our finances, and I finally gave in and told her she did not have to work. Melody wanted to have more kids; however, because of our financial situation, I didn't feel we were ready. She said the only way for our marriage to improve was if we had a child of our own. She said she needed to feel that connection. I wanted our marriage to grow stronger, but didn't know that this was the solution. Still, she demanded we try. Sometimes she'd be in tears, crying on the floor, reiterating the need to add to our brood. This went on for weeks, and her behavior shocked me. Eventually, it left me feeling helpless and made me cave—we started trying for a baby. Because of these instances, I realized my wife wanted control and didn't respect my opinion. I felt that I was being poorly treated. Melody told me what to do and when to say certain things. Our fighting started to get out of hand, and at times I wanted to give up. However, I was reminded of my parents' forty-two year marriage, and I wanted that. I remember watching my mother fight for her marriage when my father was struggling, so I wanted to do the same. The values and morals that my parents instilled in me gave me hope for my own relationship.

Even though our marriage struggled at times, we still had great moments that made me realize why we had said "I do" in the first place. One of those special moments was when Melody packed my lunch. When I ate my lunch on break, she'd include a handwritten note for me, telling me how special I was to her and that she loved me and was happy to be my wife. All the guys in my unit would give me a hard time—I think it was because they didn't receive any notes from their wives, and they were envious. I learned that it's very important to make your partner feel special when you are in a relationship. Making one another the top priority is crucial.

We had started trying for a baby in January 2007. Our relationship was still rocky, but we thought it might do us some good to go on vacation and visit Melody's other sister, Jessica, in Illinois. One afternoon during our visit, I was taking a nap. Melody came in the room and woke me up, saying she was going to take a pregnancy test. I tried to roll over and fall back asleep, but Melody came back in the room with a huge smile on her face. I immediately said, "No you're not!"

Grinning, Melody replied, "Yes, I am!"

I hugged Melody. She was pregnant with our first biological child. I was honestly ecstatic! To know that I had a child coming into this world was a miraculous feeling. When I called my mother and told her that she had her first grandchild on the way, she was on cloud nine. Even though my mother was disappointed that she wasn't involved in my wedding, having a grandkid won over my parents' approval. We then shared the good news with Melody's entire family. This was the only bright spot of our vacation.

Not long after our announcement, everything turned negative. Melody was telling me what to do and how to act around her family. I recall one time when we were eating breakfast. Her family loved eggs over easy. I however, preferred mine scrambled. Melody made a point to tell me not to *even ask* about requesting my eggs the way I liked them. Those types of little things would piss me off and only reiterated what I saw as her domineering side.

I wanted to escape this little rural town in Illinois and take her brother-in-law to Indianapolis to see a Pacers game. Melody was furious and didn't want me to spend any money. I told her I was bored in that small town and just wanted a night of fun. She frowned on it, but we went anyway. Melody's brother-in-law and I went to the Hard Rock Café for dinner and then had a great night watching the Pacers game. Because he was a pastor, he offered his counsel on how to help our marriage. Even with his advice, we still managed to fight throughout our trip, even in front of her family. It wasn't a good situation.

Though we were struggling, we headed home from vacation and started planning our next step. I needed to make sure that the foundation for my family was strong and secure. I wanted to do something more meaningful with my life, so I decided in March of 2007 that I wanted to go on active duty with the US Army. I felt ready, and thought that this would put my family and me in a better position financially. Melody gave me her blessing, and I was shipped off to training. This was our first time apart since we married, and this was going to be an adjustment. I ended up at Fort Sill Army Base in Lawton, Oklahoma, for two weeks. I processed in; I received my uniform and medical checkups, and endured physical training to equip me for the next step of Army involvement. I also went to the White Sands Training Site near Las Cruces, New Mexico, for four weeks. The drill sergeant was beyond tough with his instruction. The training was a challenge, but I wanted to emulate the drill sergeant's discipline. We had physical training every morning and ran often. Sometimes the training took us to the "field" where we learned tactics that prepared us for war. My basic training squadron worked as a team, reminding me of my Navy boot camp days.

Performing well was important to me. I had high expectations of myself, especially with the rifle qualification. The first time was tough. We moved down to White Sands Missile Range, where the goal was to lie on the ground, M-16 squared to my shoulder; then I was to aim and shoot the targets when they popped up. I did poorly my first time; I felt despondent but made sure to prepare extra hard for the next round. The next day, I became a sharpshooter, and that put me in high spirits. That experience showed me that even when I became dejected, instead of heading in a downward spiral, I *had a choice* to pick myself up and do well.

Receiving letters and photos from Melody and Tatiyana during that time also helped to boost my morale.

I completed basic training for prior service and was prepping for the next phase of my vocation. Though a lot of people saw the military as a way to pay for school, medical expenditures, and a paycheck, I saw the Army as much more. I saw it as a means to revitalize my character. I viewed it as a way to sharpen my moral fiber and polish my integrity. I was no longer a sailor; I was now a soldier in the United States Army, and I was proud to wear the uniform. As my graduation grew nearer,

Melody drove her four-month, pregnant self with Tatiyana the six hours from Phoenix to White Sands for my graduation. I had yearned for that family support, just like in my Navy days, and now I had it. When my entire unit marched to where we would reconnect with our families, I saw my beautiful wife and my sweet, 'lil Tatiyana. It took a minute to register who I was in Tatiyana's mind, but when she made the connection, she gave me that cute smile of hers. We spent time together for a few days after they saw me graduate from the first part of my training. We went to dinner in El Paso and stayed at a hotel at the White Sands Missile Range. We went to the PX to shop and spent time playing with Tatiyana. We reconnected as husband and wife. Melody and I were happy; there were no issues. We got along, laughed a lot, and had a good time. Melody told me she was proud of me; hearing that my woman supported me spoke volumes to my heart. I felt like this was a turning point; I had the will to succeed and the discipline to carry it out. I was glad to have Melody's encouragement, and I was proud to serve my country.

The second part of my training took me to Fort Jackson Army Base in South Carolina. I was stationed there for four weeks to learn my new occupation as a human resources specialist. I learned everything pertaining to the S-1, which was the main component of this department. There was a lot more classroom instruction accompanied by physical training in the morning. I received high scores on the subjects pertaining to my job. My instructor was a retired sergeant major, and she told me that she thought I would be great no matter what I set my mind to.

Being away from my family was tough this time. I faced struggles; however, one of the highlights during my training was receiving a special box in the mail from Melody. She surprised me with a sweet letter and ultrasound pictures showing I had a son on the way! I always wanted a son, because I felt like I already had a daughter in Tatiyana. I needed my new son, DeVante Gordon Angry, to even the playing field, and I thanked God for this gift.

This new information was wonderful, but it echoed the loneliness I felt being away from my family. One night during my last week of training, I felt so lonely; my fellow comrades decided to check out a local strip joint and invited me along. I called Melody to clear it with her and surprisingly, she okayed it. We got to the strip club, and I ended up spending lots of money. About half way into the night, I felt guilty, and called Melody to tell her what happened. She asked me why I had gone, even though she had given me the go ahead. This really affected her and turned into a big argument. Needless to say, I regretted my actions.

I took a long, hard look at myself and realized I wasn't showing my wife the love she deserved. I also, however, longed for Melody to show me respect. She did at times, but when I didn't feel as if I were receiving it, it affected me greatly. I felt ashamed of who I was becoming and struggled with self-esteem issues. I knew I needed to work on this, and the best thing I could do for my children was to love their mother. The value of love and honor was so important to me. At times, I think Melody and I took one another for granted. My desire was for our marriage to model what the Bible taught—that I, as a man, should love Melody as Christ loved the church; meaning, I would show her tenderness and understanding, and in turn, she would show me respect.

I loved my family and wanted to succeed in taking care of them. I graduated from the second part of my training, but no family members made it to the ceremony. Still, I felt proud of my accomplishments and all that I had learned. My military orders were for Fort Carson Army Base in Colorado Springs. I was overjoyed that we were staying in the West, which is what I wanted. When I told Melody, she was relieved, too.

My flight to Colorado Springs to report for my new assignment was a long journey. There was bad weather in Texas and my connection in Dallas was delayed, so I ended up missing my flight. I met a woman at the airport who also served in the Air Force and was trying to get to Colorado Springs. We agreed to take a flight to Denver and then rent a car and drive the rest of the way to Colorado Springs. I rented the car, and she did the driving—I slept most of the way. It was a rough evening, but when we finally arrived at Fort Carson, her husband was waiting to pick her up and take her to Peterson Air Force Base.

I reported to my assigned barracks and went through orientation. It wasn't like boot camp where we were treated like maggots and constantly yelled at in our faces. Instead, we were treated like professionals—what a refreshing feeling! I was assigned to 2-12th Infantry Regiment, 2nd Infantry Division. Upon reporting as ordered, I learned my unit was deployed to Iraq. I, however, was given permission to stay behind at Fort Carson to make the transition with Melody since she was pregnant with our first child together, who we had decided we'd name DeVante. This was also her first time being a military wife, and she was scared to be alone.

With my new orders in hand, I was given two weeks to head back to Phoenix to pick up Melody and Tatiyana and bring them to Fort Carson. On the day of the move, the movers the military had hired emptied the home we had shared for two years. We decided to keep the house and rent it to tenants. Uprooting was stressful; it also didn't help that Melody was pregnant and experiencing notable mood swings. I tried to be gracious, understanding, and let things go. We decided to drive to Fort Carson, which would take us twelve to fourteen hours. We loaded up the car and headed out of town. We drove north and spent the night at Flagstaff Fairfield Inn by Marriott. Surprisingly, for being two years old, Tatiyana handled the road trip well and slept most of the way. Early the next morning, we started our drive through northern Arizona and New Mexico. The way the sun hit the desert and mountains, and foliage was stunning—I felt like I was driving through a movie set.

We arrived in Colorado Springs around seven p.m. on that September evening in 2007 and stayed the night at the Courtyard by Marriott. While Melody and Tatiyana stayed back at the hotel, I went to the base to set up our housing and get our keys. The next morning, we opened the door to our lovely new townhome on Fort Carson Army Base. I felt like I was in the movie "We Are Soldiers," when Mel Gibson and his family arrive in their new home. Tatiyana found her room. "Oh Daddy, I love our new home!" she said to me as she hugged me. My little girl made my heart melt.

Tatiyana and I were very close. We did everything together. Some of my favorite moments happened when I came home from work every day. Tatiyana would look out the window, waiting for me. She would run down the driveway, jump into my arms, and say, "Daddy, I am so happy you're home!" Tatiyana would also come up to me just to sit on my lap and tell me how much she loved me—definitely an unbelievable way to touch a father's heart.

Melody and I talked again and agreed to proceed with my adoption of Tatiyana. When we arrived at Fort Carson in September 2007, I did a lot of my own research, because I wanted to *understand very clearly* what the adoption process was and what I needed to do to make it legit. The legal team at Fort Carson prepared the paperwork for me. I had to go through a serious criminal background check, interviews pertaining to Tatiyana—her biological father, etc. —and lots of paperwork discussing my personal history of where I lived, worked, etc. The whole process of filing papers with the courts took almost a year to complete.

One of my duties while stationed at Fort Carson was to be part of the Honor Guard. We took part in the memorial service of those who had valiantly given their lives fighting for freedom during their deployment. We marched and trained together, served alongside, and grieved with the families of these men and women. On one such occasion, I saw a grief-stricken mother of a soldier, and my heart broke for her. I hugged this anguished mother and told her that we were praying for her. I asked her to stay strong—telling her that her child had not died in vain, but sacrificially and heroically gave his life. As heart-wrenching as those moments were, I knew to count my blessings that I had not deployed with my unit.

It was Tuesday, October 30, 2007, at about four a.m. Our units were returning from Iraq, and I joined my sergeant to meet the aircraft. As we were standing there, my sergeant looked me right in the eye and said, "Angry, go home."

I looked at him quizzically and asked why.

"Your wife needs you," he said directly.

It took a minute for it to register that Melody had gone into labor. "Shut up! I don't even have my car," I said to him, frantically.

"Take my truck," Sarge said while handing me his key.

I drove to the house. Tatiyana was sleeping. Melody was in a totally different world. I took my daughter to a neighbor's house, then went back to get Melody. I was so nervous; I couldn't get anything together. That's when Melody took me by the shoulders, looked into my eyes, and forcefully said, "Shut up and get me in the car...NOW!" That woke me up, and I got her to the vehicle.

> When I saw my son's head emerge, it was the most awe-struck moment of my life.

We arrived at the hospital at 4:30 a.m., and the labor progressed. This was one of the most frightening and exhilarating experiences of my life! I started babbling, trying to take charge of things, while Melody was in labor. She just kept saying, "Shut up, don't say a word, stand there, and don't move!" When I saw my son's head emerge, it was the most awe-struck moment of my life. Watching someone be born into this world—wow, simply miraculous! The doctor handed me the scissors, and I cut the umbilical cord. They handed DeVante Gordon Angry to me at 2 p.m., all ten pounds and eight ounces! This was *my* son. I thanked God for DeVante and prayed that He would bless the life He created. I told God I

> I told God I would do everything in my power to make DeVante a man of honor.

would do everything in my power to make DeVante a man of honor.

Melody did beautifully. She had given me such a gift. I loved her more than I ever had. DeVante's birth definitely bonded us and seemed to strengthen our marriage. Melody was loving and caring, and I was doing all I could to be supportive of my wife. My parents were overjoyed when I told them their grandson had arrived. They couldn't wait to see pictures and share the news with other family members. They prayed with me over the phone and gave me a worthwhile pep talk about being a great father to my new son. Within the hour of DeVante being born, Melody rested while I went to grab dinner and drive to pick up Judy, Melody's mom, at the airport in Denver. Judy was very sweet and gracious towards me. During the two hour drive back to Colorado Springs, we made small talk. My mother-in-law expressed her gratitude for picking her up at the airport—and excitement over getting to see her daughter and new grandbaby. We focused on the well-being of my new family and on keeping my marriage strong.

The transition home from the hospital was seamless. I was no longer the bumbling fool unsure of what to do during labor. I had re-collected

 myself and become the focused individual I knew I could be. I was the planner of the family. I had everything set up at the house and ready for the baby and Melody when they arrived. Judy stayed almost a week, and that helped while I was at work. Melody was a natural, great mom with both children. Tatiyana was curious about her new little brother, but loved DeVante as much as a two-year-old could muster.

Having a new son was outstanding. I loved holding him and doting on him. I loved being Dad to both my kids. My interactions with my wife were good; Melody and I weren't really fighting, and it seemed like we were settling into a calmer routine.

In March of 2008, Melody and I planned a trip to Florida. We took the kids to Walt Disney World in Orlando and decided to visit my parents' home in Pembroke Pines. My mother answered the door with a huge smile on her face. Though my family wasn't the type to show much affection, my parents welcomed us with open arms and hugged Melody, the kids, and me—and warmly ushered us into the house. We all made small talk for about five minutes, and then my mom whisked her grandson upstairs to rock him. Her Bahamian ideology of connectedness kicked in. I had explained this to Melody before we arrived—that my mother wouldn't be being disrespectful; it was just her way of bonding with her grandson.

Over the course of our stay, my parents' true colors shined forth. My father took me into his office, my former "efficiency room," and told me how proud he was of me and that he'd raised me with the expectation that I would raise my son how I had been raised. Being back in that room served as a motivator; I had overcome its chokehold on mediocrity and was inspired to become the best father I could be. I thought he'd be a little standoffish with Melody, but my dad was the opposite. He was very cordial with her, always checking up on her to make sure she was comfortable in their home. He truly surprised me; he treated her so well and made her feel like part of the family. In turn, Melody was meek but very helpful and affable with my parents as well.

My folks were so excited to have grandchildren! My mom was so happy to have us visiting. She cooked for us, enjoyed her grandkids, and even took care of them while Melody and I shared a night on the town. My mom took Tatiyana shopping and bought her very first "Sunday dress." My dad and Tatiyana lovingly battled who was going to heaven first. This trip really delighted my heart. No matter our differences, my family showed us love and respect, and I truly appreciated that.

Though our trip was profitable, Melody and I still struggled with some underlying tension. When we returned home, we prepared for the final adoption proceedings; soon, Tatiyana would officially become my daughter. Our courthouse hearing was scheduled for 9 a.m. on April 18, 2008. When we arrived, the clerk read the docket, and the judge swore us in. She asked Melody if she gave her permission for me to become Tatiyana's father. The judge made sure Melody understood that if our marriage dissolved, I would still be equally responsible for Tatiyana's care and well-being. We both agreed

> The judge then declared that Tatiyana Isabelle Heath, almost three years old at this point, would now be Tatiyana Isabelle Angry.

and understood. The judge then declared that Tatiyana Isabelle Heath, almost three years old at this point, would now be Tatiyana Isabelle Angry.

We were *officially* a family. We went out to breakfast to celebrate, and I couldn't keep my eyes off *my* daughter. I had received another incredible gift from God, and I realized that she too had received a gift—the gift of a father. Tatiyana no longer had to wonder who her dad was.

As the weeks went on, tension started to rebuild. I was getting used to my new change of command. My new boss was very tough on me, and my job became very demanding. Melody and I still had our ups and downs, but we started to become more like roommates than husband

and wife. Our communication suffered more, and it got to the point where I would volunteer to work extra shifts so I didn't have to go home to what felt like a loveless marriage.

One day, in March 2008 while at the 2-12IN family awareness rally and post-deployment fair, I met a fellow soldier, DeMarcus Hysten. We made small talk and connected instantly. In a short amount of time, we became fast friends. Early on, DeMarcus pinpointed some of my struggles. We opened up to one another about the challenges we faced, and he jokingly told me that "I was his Bubba and he was my Gump."

As problems arose in my personal life, DeMarcus became my go-to guy. He heard my heart when I shared with him about my marriage. I would tell him about the ups and downs and how I struggled to receive Melody's respect. Her lack of faith in me took its toll and began to affect every area of my life. DeMarcus and his wife, Tiffany, invited Melody and me to a marriage retreat in Boulder that was sponsored by the Army. I tried to soak in all the advice I could, but for Melody, the retreat didn't seem effective. She didn't want to communicate with me. I confided more in DeMarcus at the couples' retreat about the condition of my marriage. Those talks deepened our friendship. We started to hang out with DeMarcus and Tiffany on a regular basis. They'd come over and witness Melody and my interactions and the fighting that took place in our home. When it became too much, I'd go to their house as a reprieve. DeMarcus and I would hang out in his basement. He would sing and play his piano, all the while encouraging me to be the best dad and husband I could be.

Melody told me she was overwhelmed being home with the kids all day and needed some alone time. I watched the kids in the evenings so she could have a break. She was a good mom, so I saw no problem giving her a night off. During this time, my unit was preparing to deploy to Afghanistan. I had many meetings with my commander, Michael Pearl, and sergeant major, Charles Sasser. They both saw what I was going through and told me they needed a fighting soldier. Given my circumstances, I wasn't that. They gave me thirty days to get things in order and get motivated. If I was unable to handle it, they told me to let them know.

One day, when I came home from the "field" on break, I found Melody in the living room, crying.

"Melody, what's wrong?" I asked, concerned. I knew things were tense with us, but I didn't know what was going on with her thinking.

She was quiet.

I'm not certain what prompted me, but I asked her, "What, did you cheat on me or something?"

Melody looked at me and began to cry again.

I had all these questions going through my head. What? When? Who? Where? *Melody had cheated on me. I knew our marriage was in shambles, but I wasn't ready to give up.* We had just solidified our family weeks before when I had officially adopted Tatiyana. What was going on? I knew Melody wasn't happy in our marriage. She told me she struggled with feeling like she rushed into marriage and didn't feel devoted to me anymore. It was like she was looking for a way out—she wanted me to pull the trigger and end things. Even though Melody broke my heart, and my anger and hurt were obvious, my love for her remained strong.

My mind was in a whirlwind. My life was falling apart. The difficulties of my broken marriage and the rigorous Army training became a real struggle. I didn't know what to do. I sought counsel at a local church, but didn't feel comfortable there. One day, I met a guy at a Blockbuster video store near my house, and we struck up a conversation. He told me about this large, non-denominational church called New Life, and I decided to go visit. I didn't realize until afterwards that it was a church that was going through its share of issues. The long-term pastor had left in disgrace, and there had been a shooting incident where people were wounded and killed. Why did I attend this church? I enjoyed the service, and it was a bright spot being away from the base and the utter chaos that was my life. I listened to my heart and the small comfort I received, and continued to attend.

The replacement pastor was Brady Boyd. One of his messages addressed the shootings that had taken place at the church. He shared how both the families of the shooters and the victims had come face to face and overcame their disputes. Pastor Boyd's message inspired me to fight for my marriage and to hold God's hand while I figured out the direction for my life. Like Mr. White at Promise Keepers and Pastor Don at CCV, Pastor Boyd ignited a part of my heart that wanted me to become more. I desired to become a better man and a better soldier. Melody and my family went to the services with me. She heard the same messages I did, but was unaffected by them. Melody shut down and wouldn't communicate with me.

Though my desires were commendable, the reality was, life was arduous. I remembered how I rose to the occasion and served during an oppressive time in war while in the Navy. I had to be brave then. I battled cancer, and death was at my doorstep; but I persevered and battled on. I once had the support of a wonderful woman and a loving family. But now? Now I was serving in the Army, and I didn't feel courageous. I felt broken, and life only got more difficult with each new blow.

My failing marriage and the loss of my support system were detrimental in more ways than one. I learned that my cancer might have returned, and I was scheduled for surgery. Things got so bad that I called DeMarcus one night crying. It was May 28, 2008, and I told him that Melody had taken my kids and left me. It was four days before I was to have my procedure. DeMarcus was dumbfounded, and I could tell his heart broke for me.

A familiar nemesis from my earlier days, depression, crept in uninvited and wreaked havoc on my everyday life. When it did, nothing mattered to me. I sought counsel from my good friend, Meg Britton. She counseled me while her husband, Tim, spent hours praying with me over the phone. I considered them to be my spiritual mom and pop. One evening, I met up with Tim and Meg at their home, high in the mountains above Manitou Springs, Colorado, and decided to hear what they had to say about Melody's and my situation. As I sat there and poured out my heart and many tears concerning our relationship and what had transpired, I could feel their unconditional love and acceptance for us. The Britton's recognized that Melody and I were two broken people who continued to hurt one another, and that I was the only one willing to make the changes and sacrifices necessary to save our family. Tim and Meg encouraged me to show Christ's unconditional love to Melody—keeping the lines of communication open and continuing to be a responsible father to my children.

I called Melody constantly and wrote letters often. She was back in Leavenworth, Washington, staying with her parents. I sent her flowers and begged for her to accept me again, and asked her repeatedly not to break up our family. I did everything in my power to let Melody know I loved her and wanted her to come home. Despite my best efforts, our marriage deteriorated over the next few months until Melody decided to file for divorce.

I felt like a failure. I remembered the oppositions my parents faced, and how my mother had been an advocate for her marriage. She and my dad had battled the storms together and survived; why couldn't Melody and I do the same? My mother took this moment to have one of those "come to Jesus" talks with her son. She said to me, "Travis, I love you. You need to let this go. God has greater plans for you. You need to let this be and move forward." I took her advice and tried to let go.

My commander and I came to the conclusion that I wasn't in the right frame of mind, and it was best that I didn't deploy. Because I didn't complete my four years in the Army, I was given a general discharge under honorable conditions. Most people, I felt, regardless of the opposition, would have handled themselves better. Most would have focused on their duties and put themselves on the backburner. Unfortunately, I wasn't that soldier, and these circumstances ended my Army career. I, however, will always be indebted to the Army for the opportunities they afforded my family and for the character traits they instilled in me to become a better man.

I made the decision to head back to Phoenix and change focus. When I returned, the first thing I did was seek counseling at CCV. Scott Harris, the family ministries director at CCV, counseled me. I poured out my heart to him about my impending divorce and separation from Melody and my kids. Scott saw the heaviness that I carried in my heart. I realized it was easy to play the "blame game," attacking myself for the failure of my marriage, and listen to the negative talk that crept in. Though I struggled, Scott would pray with me and challenge me to get better. We met weekly. Even during this difficult time, Scott helped me to focus on becoming the best man I could be. He reassured me that even though I didn't feel it, God loved me unconditionally. Despite all that was happening in my life, I wanted God to help me become that courageous man and selfless leader and lover. Scott helped me regain my footing on that spiritual foundation; he became a good friend through my healing process.

As I healed, I decided I wanted to get involved with the children's ministry at CCV. I realized that I could make a positive difference not only in my life, but also in the lives of my children and others. Despite the scars that tried to form when our divorce finalized in August 2009, I decided that I needed to be positive and uplifting to those who mattered most to me. I realized it was time for me to "let go and let God," and work at becoming the best version of myself I could. I went back to school and worked full time with the IRS. By January, 2010, I felt like a new man. I had let go of all the negative feelings I had harbored in my heart. Though I was still working on forgiving Melody, I focused on doing well for my kids. While I don't want to divulge all of the details of Melody's challenges, it became clear over time that I would need to step up to the plate to care for our children. Melody's personal challenges became too great a responsibility for her to handle, and my kids needed me.

It was very scary to me at first, because this was an unknown situation. For the first time, I was about to become a parent on my own.

As I reflected on the storms I faced, I realized the military and my battle with cancer had given me the strength to overcome monumental obstacles in life. The resilience, discipline, and endurance I had discovered through these trials would provide me with the fortitude I needed in becoming a fulltime, single father in May of 2010.

I had to meet Melody in Chicago to get the kids. I walked into the hotel, and when I saw my kids, it hit me: *I was going back to Arizona to be a fulltime dad.* I had already put certain things in place: daycare, schools, church, a stocked refrigerator, etc. But when we were coming back, the first moment of realization came for me when we were at thirty-five thousand feet in the air, and Tatiyana looked at me and said, "I love you, Daddy. I can't wait to get back to Arizona." That made it real.

I took my job as a fulltime father seriously from the get-go. When we got back to Arizona, I took them to get haircuts and style up, so they could *look and feel good.* When I dropped them off at school on their first day, they cried because *they didn't want me to leave.* They had already gone through enough separation, and didn't want to let me out of their sight. The school director made me leave, even with the kids screaming. We did this for a week or two until they adjusted.

Then, I got to start experiencing their developmental stages—for example, I got to see my daughter enter kindergarten. While walking in line for her classroom, something hit me: I realized she felt safe. I realized

the depth of my role, in making sure she had the security necessary to live a healthy life.

Once my kids had *security*, they felt *comfortable and safe*. Then, *they could live their lives*. I realized that I am a very loving and a disciplinary father—and that kid's need both.

I learned that there are always challenges in parenting. It makes you better and holds you accountable. Parenthood is not designed to be a smooth ride. You will fail and succeed at the same time, along with your kids.

> I learned that there are always challenges in parenting. It makes you better and holds you accountable. Parenthood is not designed to be a smooth ride. You will fail and succeed at the same time, along with your kids.

I had to adjust in more ways than I imagined. At one point, I told myself, "Oh my gosh; I'm going to raise a *daughter? Travis Angry*, who was on the streets of Miami? *I'm* going to raise a *little girl?*" My son was easy. My daughter…was a daughter. She was very affectionate. I had never been an affectionate man because it wasn't modeled for me from my parents. So, my little girl burst my shell and allowed herself to come in. Instead sitting at home watching ESPN, I had a little girl cuddling up with her dad and breaking whatever shell I had around me.

I also learned that I'm not a cook. *I'm old school*. My mom had kicked my brothers and me out of the kitchen. We'd work in the yard or garage, but making food was not something I wanted to do. So providing meals for my children was a challenge in and of itself.

Additionally, I would learn that one of my biggest challenges—my cancer—wasn't done with me yet. I endured additional treatments in 2011 and 2012. Undergoing chemotherapy while serving as a fulltime single father certainly brought unique challenges, but I persevered.

The beautiful part of this experience was growing through my church—having a support system that allowed us to grow while impacting me to be the dad that God had appointed me to be.

This colossal incident in my life—becoming a fulltime, single father—opened my eyes to the youth culture around me. Of all the "unpleasantries" that could affect these young people, the impact of broken homes had to be one of the greatest. More than ever, it became clear to me that our society needs willing parents who will step up and show these kids love, hope, and responsibility. These attributes afford youngsters the opportunity to succeed. Today, that's why I'm sharing my story. My hope is to inspire our youth culture to reach their aspirations. I want to motivate adults to become role models. Just like I had in my life, I want adults to take the time and invest in our young people. I want those adults to hold adolescents accountable for their actions and spur them on toward greater feats. Just imagine, if others took this call to action seriously, the results could be astronomical...

CHAPTER 6

EDUCATION

*"If you are going to achieve excellence in big things, you develop the habit
in little matters. Excellence is not an exception, it is a prevailing attitude."*
—Colin Powell

While I had started college during my marriage, I found the motivation to finish after my divorce. In the winter of 2008, I had an epiphany: *I needed to finish my education.* In fact, I was so motivated to finish that I suddenly called my counselor and said, "Get me back in class." I also promised to myself that I would not remarry until I had received my degree. The economy was struggling, and it was very difficult to find jobs without a degree; I didn't want this to hold me back any longer.

As I made this shift to focus on my education, I thought about my dad, and how much he had persevered to succeed. My father, Raymond Angry, Sr., was living proof that one could reach his aspirations—as I strove to do. Despite coming from an oppressive upbringing in the cotton fields of Albany, Georgia, Dad had a vision. As I mentioned previously, day after day as he toiled away under the hot sun picking cotton, he'd tell himself that things were going to change and that things were going to get better. He believed that there was more to life than just cotton picking—more to life than just being someone's slave, day in and day out. My father swore to himself that he would revolutionize his world and give his future family a chance at a different life. The gateway to affording this dream was to get an education. My dad believed what Horace Mann once wrote: "A human being is not attaining his full heights until he is educated." Dad would also do whatever it took to live up to Gilbert J. Chersterson's philosophy that "education is simply the soul of a society as it passes from one generation to another." My father walked the road of schooling; he toiled, sacrificed, and dedicated himself to education so as to provide a better life for his family. Dr. Raymond Angry, Sr., led by example. He was a prime example that education could bring valuable rewards. He was the first one in his family to graduate from college. He obtained his bachelor's in sociology and master's in criminal justice. He went on to receive his Ph.D. in education as well. Dad became a leadership and education professor at Nova Southeastern University and a dynamic public speaker. *My father was a role model.* He stood out as a pillar of the community; he broke a familial cycle that was once bound by hardship. He opened doors that motivated others to follow. He set the bar high and expected his children to grasp the significance and value of learning. He motivated me to do the same.

As I reentered college, I also thought about my education throughout my life. I had felt like the black sheep of the family. Being the second born, I believed I lived in the shadow of my older brother. While Raymond Jr. was busy pursuing his dream as a talented musician, I remained "stuck." The overwhelming feeling that I wouldn't amount to anything, no matter how hard I tried, weighed heavily on my heart. Those fears and insecurities first manifested themselves at an early age.

What I didn't explain earlier in the story is that I had also developed a learning disability, although it was not diagnosed until I was an adult in college. That learning disability had affected me in ways that only became clear looking back. When I attended kindergarten through sixth grade at Hibiscus Elementary School in Miami, Florida, I had to go to a "resource room" for help in math and reading. All the "misfits," as I dubbed us, were sent to Mrs. Cathlit who specialized in helping kids like me to learn how to grasp reading and math. I knew that I wasn't smart. However, the only respite I had as a youngster was that Mrs. Cathlit encouraged her students. She saw my potential and expressed kindness. Our reward for completing the class was a pool party every summer at her home. This was significant because she showed us that even if others treated us as "misfits," we were still worthy of her love. Junior high and high school had produced its ups and downs, too. I struggled, but my only reprieve was history class. Something about the stories of the past resonated with me. I loved to learn about presidents and the Constitution. Our country wasn't that old, but it had undergone tremendous obstacles—wars, catastrophes, the fight for freedom. I guess in my own way, I could identify with its struggles.

Later I remember going to school in Pembroke Pines, trying to make my transition to a new place and school as smoothly as possible. It was January 1992, and I was eighteen years old. I longed for acceptance and to be the best. My hopes were dashed when I struggled to keep focus on the big picture. As my younger brothers, Dexter and Jason made their niche in this world; I was faced with a mêlée of self that hindered my progress.

> Maybe some of you reading this book can identify with what I am saying. *I was an ordinary kid with ordinary abilities.*

Maybe some of you reading this book can identify with what I am saying. *I was an ordinary kid with ordinary abilities.* As hard as I tried, my performance wasn't top notch. My dad would be on me about getting good grades. Something inside me longed to please him, to make my parents proud. I craved my father's attention and longed for him to look at me the way he looked at my brothers. *However, it seemed the harder I tried, the more I screwed up.*

I had started out well in my classes. I had listened attentively to what the teacher taught and did my best to apply it. However, when it came time to test my knowledge, I'd fail. This greatly affected my self-confidence as an adolescent and made me wonder if I was truly stupid. Was I that "misfit" I felt like in grade school? I knew there was more depth to me, but the positives didn't shine. Instead, my shortcomings were highlighted to my parents, and Dad frequently looked at me disapprovingly.

I struggled to receive approval and adoration—to find the connection that would bond my father and me. Education was the link, but since my confidence had waned, I became less eager about learning.

I had had other distractions besides my learning disability. I also couldn't stay focused on my education because I was distracted by my search *I didn't know then that all my searching, seeking, and neediness were actually creating the very thing I didn't want—rejection. I didn't understand that dynamic and what that was doing to me. I was hurting myself without even knowing it.*

This rejection had fueled my self-loathing. My adolescent mind started to believe I was pathetic. I was failing in all directions of my life: school, girls, and low self-esteem. I had no idea where I was going in my life. I was technically a senior in high school at this point and needing to think about college and career goals. However, because I was failing, school was the last thing on my mind. What was the point in trying? I skipped school and wandered about aimlessly. I felt like a nomad—roaming from place to place, but uncertain what the search would bring.

I didn't know then that all my searching, seeking, and neediness were actually creating the very thing I didn't want—rejection. I didn't understand that dynamic and what that was doing to me. I was hurting myself without even knowing it.

My guidance counselor tried to talk and encourage me, but it was too late. I had mentally checked out. The principal took action and tried to discipline me; however, it didn't do any good. I was transferred to an adult education school, but I repeated the same pattern of behavior at my new school. My parents were upset and disappointed, but I didn't care. I felt frustrated and placed blame on them for why I was failing. At this point, no matter what anyone said, it was no use.

I couldn't take it anymore; I had decided to drop out of school. My father was heartbroken and furious with me. Dad and I were at odds all the time, and my mother had to play referee.

Dad had locked me out of the house and told me to be productive. I tried to get a job and maintain it; however, for whatever reason, I couldn't keep one very long. I wandered about without direction, without purpose. I continued to feel insignificant. I was officially a high school dropout and had lost my parents' confidence in me. I was now headed down a path of self-destruction. I lacked discipline and focus.

How did I end up here? I thought at the time. I had come from a successful family, so why did I feel like such a loser? I expressed my concerns to my mother, and she reiterated her belief in me. During that confusing time, my mother and I formed a deeper bond. As I sought direction for my life, my mother was my inspiration. As Bahamian born, my mother had struggled to learn proper English in the states. During my own search for significance, my mother set an example for me. Now that her sons were older, she took time to invest her dreams, her education. I watched my mother work toward getting her G.E.D. with my father's help. Once she received it, she went on to Florida Memorial College and received her bachelor's of science degree.

Though I was proud of my mother, I still had no interest in school. I didn't have a job and spent most of my time living on the streets. I ran with a gang and hustled people for money and rides. I stole from family and being a "misfit" became my way of life. It wasn't until 9/11 that I had an epiphany. I took a hard look at myself and detested the person I had become. I watched my mother pursue her education and get her master's degree in elementary education from Nova Southeastern University—an educational specialist degree in the area of reading—and even pursue her doctorate of education in instructional leadership with a specialization in reading. If my mother could have the drive and know-how, what was stopping me?

I know that many young people get caught up in the "now" and think that education is a waste of time. Many think teachers are there to bore students with useless information and keep them from having a life of fun. If you are a student reading this, you may think that you sit in the classroom, day in and day out, with your mind wondering, *Is this all worth it?* I was that person; I dreaded school and wanted to know what else was out there.

Eventually, I had to realize that if I really wanted to get somewhere in life, I needed a good education. I wanted to become something more, and the Navy helped me do that. I had prepared for the G.E.D. and took the exam at the Navy College Office. I thought about all that I had put my parents through to this point. I thought about my dad's hardcore instruction on how to succeed and my mother's quiet example that spoke volumes to me. It was my turn to take that step, make my father proud, and make myself successful. The only way I could officially do that was by passing this test. That is what stood between me and my military career. When the results came back, I was nervous. Given my poor history of test taking, I was uncertain what the outcome would be. I ran down to the Navy College Office, and a secretary showed me the results: a passing score! I was now *officially* a high school graduate! For the first time in a long time, I was proud of myself. I *knew* I was smart and had potential to do great things.

I can relate to you young people reading this. Your parents place high expectations on you to achieve the best and to be the best, right? You long to please them, but you also understand that the pressures don't help. After all, you are only human. I felt the same way. I never allowed myself to think I'd be college bound. I didn't think I was *worthy*. I thought I was dumb, stupid, and everyone knew it. But guess what? I changed my thinking. I had a foundation to build from.

I looked for role models, and at the time, Secretary of State Colin Powell was mine. His leadership skills made me want to emulate him. He spoke with such distinction and poise. I read everything I could about Colin Powell and realized that his speaking abilities ignited the natural talent I felt I potentially possessed.

Later, I had attended Mesa Community College. I only enrolled in one class because I still had fears that I would fail. I figured I'd start off slow and go from there. I passed that English class with a B and was happy! It helped to build my confidence.

Eventually, I ended up moving into a new home and transferred to Glendale Community College. I went to orientation and, for the first time, felt excited to be a student again. My perspective from adolescence had shifted. I now looked at myself as a man with potential and drive. I studied hard and passed my classes. I would look at my college transcripts and saw that my credits were building. My relationship with my father improved because I was no longer a lost soul—I had direction in my life. I loved giving him updates on my progress and what I was learning; he in turn gave me advice on how to continue to walk the road of schooling successfully. Looking back, I remember when my dad would tell me and my friends *time and time again* that education was *the most important* thing. Then, I thought his lectures were a drag, but later I could see the validity in his words.

I had entered a program through vocational rehab for disabled veterans like myself (for service-connected disabilities from my back injury and battle with cancer). I received veterans' benefits, and had a helpful guidance counselor with whom I'd share my aspirations. I had completed my first semester at Glendale Community College, and in December 2006, I received an acceptance letter from Arizona State University saying I had enough credits to transfer to their school.

As a Sun Devil, a student at ASU, I did more than just attend classes. I was building my knowledge of social issues and becoming aware of their effects on our society. I read books in addition to the ones my professors assigned. My love of history was reignited, and I again studied the Constitution and became fascinated by the freedom we possess. I learned that although we now live in an age of technology, our nation's past is what helped shape who I was becoming. The sacrifices of many of our country's greatest heroes and heroines paved the way for me to dream big.

I was focused on earning my bachelor's degree in public administration. Because I loved serving people, I wanted to work in government or public service. I was a people person and wanted to use my military experience as a human resource specialist to help others. I knew I needed a plan; I had to adopt a good attitude, have confidence, and continue my mission to finish college. I knew there would be bumps in the road that would challenge me in the process, but I needed to stay consistent and not give up.

I eventually switched to online courses at the University of Phoenix in August of 2007, because I had moved to active duty with the Army. At the time, my plate was full—I was a dad, husband, soldier, breadwinner, and full-time student. Online courses worked for me because the classes didn't have final exams. Many challenges arose that tried to derail my efforts of finishing school. During the time I was at University of Phoenix, I went through my separation and divorce, and I was serving my country while preparing to deploy overseas. In 2008, as a single dad, I re-enrolled with the newfound goal of finishing school, once and for all.

I remember Dad calling me in July 2010, early in the morning, saying that my mom had passed from cancer. My mother had become one of my closest confidantes, and losing her was extremely difficult. I wore the numbness like a garb. I was closer to her than my father, and as I reflected back, I felt I didn't do enough to show her that I loved her. That took a toll on my schooling. However, despite my heartache, I persisted with my studies. I envisioned my mom at the table studying, night after night. Her spirit gave me the courage to continue my educational fight.

Months later, I had a conversation with my father that stuck with me. Dad would often talk about his readiness to reunite with my mother in the next life. He also told me, "Travis, I'll be out of here one day, and I need you to be strong for our family. You are my light and rock. I need you to help Raymond take care of your little brothers." My dad's charge spoke volumes to me, and I vowed to do what I could.

My finance counselor, Meghan Dolberg, and my academic counselor, Meghan Brown, at the University of Phoenix, could not believe I still kept my focus and completed my coursework despite my grief. I would still look at my transcripts and keep tabs on how I was doing. I had adopted the motto of Larry Fitzgerald, who played for the Arizona Cardinals: "Faith, focus, and finish." I saw that I only had one semester to go; the finish line was in sight. I called my father and left him a message to give him the good news that his son was going to be graduating in the fall of 2011. Not long after, in the June of 2011, my youngest brother, Jason, called early in the morning and told me that my dad had died from complications associated with his diabetes. The news was indeed hard, but because of the conversations we had previously, I was a little more prepared for his death.

Losing my parents was indeed excruciatingly painful. Looking back, I realize that the legacy my parents aimed to build would aid me in my own journey. Though my military career didn't pan out as I had hoped, I realized there was still hope for me. Cancer couldn't keep me down, and neither could a failed marriage. My parents' death could have crushed me, but it only motivated me more to set my sights high and regain fortitude. They taught me about love, sacrifice, education, and perseverance under trial. They set the standards for life—spiritually and morally. They provided me with a road map for marriage, family, how to be a good father, and how to set a good example.

Despite all my challenges, I took my parents' advice. Every day, I would sit at my computer, dedicating hour after hour to my online courses. *Nothing* was going to stop me from finishing school. *"Faith, focus, and finish"* were my motivators. I would finish my degree in my parents' honor.

In September 2011, I received a surprising phone call from my academic counselor, Meghan Brown. *"Mr. Angry, you can now register for commencement in November of 2011. You will be walking across the University of Phoenix Stadium as a college graduate. Congratulations!"*

When I hung up the phone, tears rolled down my cheeks. What I believed could never be possible in my lifetime had come to fruition: Travis Angry was now a college graduate! I was very humbled. Everything had come full circle; because of those who believed in me and because of the belief I had in myself, the culmination of success was realized.

On November 12, 2011, Veterans Day weekend, I walked into this massive stadium at the University of Phoenix, ready to graduate from college. As I stood in line waiting to march out onto the floor, I couldn't help but think of both of my parents and all that they had achieved when it came to education. As I stood there, I came across a quote displayed on the tunnel of the stadium walls. Lou Holtz, former Notre Dame Head Coach and current ESPN analyst of college football said, *"Ability is what you're capable of doing. Motivation determines what you do. Attitude determines how well you do it."* This was a timely message for me, and I wrote down these valuable words. As the other graduates and I walked onto the field, I soaked it all in. This was a spotlight moment. In this very place, Larry Fitzgerald had caught a touchdown pass while playing for the Cardinals. Now, I walked across that stage. I teared up as I saw my children smiling at me. Travis Angry's efforts were shining: making my parents, children, and siblings proud. Afterward, my closest family and friends helped me celebrate this milestone at the beautiful Renaissance Hotel & Spa in Glendale, Arizona, with a graduation and business luncheon. I gave a speech, which launched my new career as a motivational speaker (see Appendix in this book for the transcript).

Travis with his University of Phoenix graduating class.

Travis receiving his diploma; shaking hands with the Uniiversity President.

Travis is a University of Phoenix graduate!

Travis celebrating his achievement with the Angry family.

Together with my brothers, to this day, we continue our parents' legacy. I am a new professional with an exciting vision for the future. I'm also currently enrolled in University of Phoenix's MBA program. I still place a very high value on education and consider myself a lifelong learner. In my own way, I carry the torch and light the way to a better future. I use my personal story to inspire youth and their parents. My mission is to impact our youth culture for positive change. I help young people to know that when they find their passion, it will fuel their purpose in life. If you love what you do, this will help you succeed. My organization, *CHANGE: If I Can, You Can*, is a movement that can revitalize America and take our youth culture to new heights.

A Tribute to My Parents
Dr. Raymond Angry, Sr., and Dr. Glenburia Angry

God places a good woman in your life. It's up to you to extend your hand out and allow her to come in and have faith that God will bless you in doing so.
—Travis Angry

As I discussed previously, their story was simple but like an award-winning novel. My dad, a sales clerk in a shoe store, and my mom, the unsuspecting customer. She was no longer a woman just in search of shoes—she was the starring lead in a love story unfolding…a courtship began and a love blossomed.

You could see it in his eyes. Each day he lived, it was there…it was in her eyes as well. Love: It was pure, and it was of value. It was amazing to watch them talk, to watch them grow together…my parents had truly built an incredible foundation of love, and it was obvious in their lives together. My father would go the extra mile to show my mom his love;

and, although she was quiet in her words, my mom's love for my dad was shown through action. It was evident to all.

My mom was a homemaker; she lovingly made our home a safe haven and refuge. My dad was first in her heart, then her boys. My brothers and I were well aware of this hierarchy. Nothing could come between their love; but when the storms raged, the love of Jesus Christ was the glue that kept them together. My mother would wake in the early morning, an hour before my dad had to get up. She would iron his clothes and fix him a good breakfast before he headed off to work. Dad was prepared for a successful day, because my mother sent him off in a loving way. In our society, many downgrade the value on that type of marriage; the focus is on self and not investing in our partner. Not my parents—it was all about their marriage and leaning on God's direction for their lives.

My four brothers and I were raised in the city, but it felt like we were being raised in the sweet secret of Georgia… except as youngsters it felt like my dad worked us as he had in the cotton fields. My parents were strict but very loving in their own ways. The most important gift they gave me and my brothers was their constant love and devotion. Being a stay-at-home mom with four boys wasn't easy—it was a challenge, make no mistake about it. My mother had a loud voice, and when my brothers and I got into trouble, we felt it. She'd have us clean the house from top to bottom and expected the best out of us. However, we also felt comfortable and secure with her. Like the centerpiece of a beautifully, decorated table that completes everything, that was my mama. She was the backbone of our family. My mother and I were very close, and I believe that is why I am so much closer to her side of the family. Her grace and love were enduring, and I felt it every day of my life. We spent lots of time together; I would drive her to where she needed to go. Our car rides became like therapy sessions; they were where I received all my knowledge regarding God, family, and women.

Yes, my mother talked to me about women. She set the standards and told me never to settle for less than the best. She would tell me to find a woman who was into me—one who would treat me with love, dignity, and respect. In turn, she would tell me to make sure I made the woman in my life feel special, and that God would reward me for treasuring her. No, there aren't many women in our culture like my mother. We live in a more career-driven society. I thank my dear mother for showing my brothers and me consistent love, and how to weather the storms and stand strong.

My father and I bumped heads often, but I admired him for being a great man of honor. As I reflect back, we still had special moments together. We bonded over our love of sports. Every Sunday afternoon, we'd watch football after church. The Miami Dolphins were our favorite team; Dan Marino was my favorite quarterback even though Dad wasn't too fond of him. When he missed a play, Dad would jokingly roast me for being a Dan Marino fan. Though it hurt my feelings, it was these times with my dad that helped me to develop a good-natured and competitive spirit.

The special moments I had with my dad are bright spots in my world. We joked about life and things in general, both loved my mother's cooking, and both vied for her attention. I believe I possess the talents and gifts I do because of my father. I was the archetype of my father, because growing up, I wanted to be the best, I wanted to own the most, and I wanted to exceed my brothers' achievements.

That's who my father was: a man who possessed confidence and great potential. He obtained his Ph.D. in education (his greatest achievement inspired us all), but most importantly, he motivated me in every way possible. I longed for his acceptance in everything I did, but he wanted me to define my own path, make my own decisions. My father was a character; he wasn't afraid to express himself. He wanted others, especially his family, to know how much he loved God and how much he loved his wife.

Just like my father, my mother broke the cycle and endured hardships to achieve the highest level of education. While battling cancer, my mother pursued her Ph.D. She'd lie there in her hospital bed, working on assignments. Day in and day out, she did this, until one day, she laid there unconscious, unable to do anymore. My mother was a fighter and victorious to the very end.

I knew that the time was coming when I would receive those phone calls. I tried my best to prepare, but one can never fully prepare for death. My phone rang at five o'clock in the morning in June 2010—it was my father. He had a calm voice, and with the softest words, he told me my mother had passed and that he was okay. I told my dad I loved him and that he had done his best for the forty-two years of their marriage. When I hang up the phone, I collapsed on my bed and took myself mentally to heaven to say my goodbyes. Two days later, my dad called again, this time crying. He told me that Nova Southeastern University had awarded my mother her Ph.D. in education and was now known as Dr. Glenburia Angry.

When I hung up the phone, all I could do was smile. I was a proud son, and I was in awe of my mother. A woman, who had once come from the Bahamian islands, didn't speak proper English, was a stay-at-home mom, and was now receiving her Ph.D., through her struggles, she had achieved excellence.

My mother's funeral was difficult but heartfelt. My dad shocked everyone when he stood up to speak and say his final goodbye. He went to the microphone and started to sing "Because She Lives." It was moving. As he spoke about his love for my mother, everyone in the church was empowered by his words. My dad paid quite a tribute to my mother that day. In my heart, I was thankful. It was tough to have to mourn the loss of my mother, but I take comfort in the fact that she's in a better place.

My youngest brother, Jason, took care of my parents while they were sick, and exemplified great courage through a devastating ordeal. I felt bad for not being there to help with my parents, but they understood I had a life in Arizona where I was raising both of my kids. My parents always told me to focus on them and to succeed as a father. Both of my parents developed a bond with their grandchildren. Even though I had adopted Tatiyana, they had accepted her as flesh and blood. After my mother's funeral, my dad told Tatiyana to always hold her grandmother's memory in her heart. To this day, Tatiyana still talks about her. DeVante never had that chance to know his grandmother, but she held DeVante in her arms as an infant and loved him so! DeVante was more of a crier and didn't like my father to hold him. However, the day we said goodbye, DeVante walked over to his grandfather and gave him a big hug…it was a special moment because that was the last time DeVante would ever embrace his granddad.

When my mother passed, my father was ready to go. My little brother, Jason, said Dad would cry himself to sleep. He'd constantly talk about leaving this life and reuniting with his wife. I tried to get him to focus on other things, but he told me that until I found a woman like my mother and had been with her through thick and thin for forty-two years, I would never understand why he felt the urgency he did.

During one of my last conversations with my dad before he passed, we talked about his afterlife and what he expected of me. He told me to take care of myself, love God with all of my heart, and lean on His understanding for the direction of my life. He told me to invest in education and to take good care of his grandkids, DeVante and Tatiyana. As we sat at Cracker Barrel, his favorite place to eat breakfast, I told my father that I was going to raise my children like he raised me. I told him I was a great man because of him. As we looked at each other face to face, I knew this was the last time I'd see my father alive. I said, "I love you, Dad," and he responded with, "I love you, Son. Stay strong for your brothers. There's no need to cry. It doesn't matter which way in life I go. Either way, I win, because I'm a Christ follower." I was at peace, and I knew I had to stay steadfast.

In June of 2011, when Jason called me and told me my dad got his wish—he was now united with his beloved bride—I was grief-stricken but at peace. I knew my dad was where he wanted to be.

One day, I will reunite with my parents in heaven. Because of their guidance and example, the best gift I ever gave to my parents was the commitment I made to Christ. Through my story, I hope people will realize that time in this life is short and that family is truly precious. We need to take the time to make those connections and lay a strong foundation for greatness. For now, Jeremiah 29:11 has become my personal mantra: *"For I know the plans I have for you," declares the* LORD, *"plans to prosper you and not to harm you, plans to give you hope and a future." Because of this promise, my future looks bright, and my parents continue to inspire me because their spirits live on.*

Until we meet again, Mom and Dad, I love you... —Travis

CHAPTER 7

A Message to Parents, Educators, and Community Members

"If you can dream it, then you can achieve it. You will get all you want in life if you help enough other people get what they want."
—Zig Ziglar

In November 2011, *Change: If I Can, You Can,* an inspirational and motivational youth outreach project, was launched. As part of the backbone of this project, the story you are currently reading was put to book form with the goal of motivating and inspiring today's youth as they deal with various circumstances. Since today's youth face significant challenges— including childhood obesity, bullying, teen pregnancy, and

dropping out of school—many of these young people suffer from low self-esteem and involvement with drugs or even gangs. Many young people lack direction and fall into a vicious cycle of self-doubt and negative consequences. This movement will be a resource to aid parents, educators, and other youth-focused groups. The mission of *Change: If I Can, You Can,* is to motivate and inspire participants to think, feel, and dream about ways to better their own lives. When youth are empowered, they can also greatly influence their surrounding communities and legislation on a national and global scale.

If you are a youth reading this, I think you will find value in understanding the state of things today, so that you can initiate change. So please don't let the title of this chapter dissuade you from reading more.

As an adult, when you look back on your own life and hear the word "childhood," what do you think? Are you remembering happy moments with your family, spending quality time together, or do you dread these reveries because it was an unpleasant time of relentless teasing and abuse? The perspective that you relate to the most gives you a glimpse into the world of how the next generation is being shaped. Most people in our grandparents' generation were from a two-parent home—with a dad working and a mom taking care of the family. Children were respectful and did as they were told. Dad was the head of the household, and reverence was given to that role. Today, we have a society drowning in chaos—filled with broken spirits and broken families. Jamy Beaton, a concerned mother and a friend of mine, shared her observation with me: "We are living in a world where 'respect your elders' is as foreign as black and white television and 8 tracks." Jamy's statement rings true; it seems as if respect for self and respect for others has been thrown out the window.

It is so vital for you as parents to set the example for your children at an early age to become productive members of society. What they learn in the classroom needs to be reinforced at home and vice versa. Putting character qualities such as respect, self-control, and responsibility into practice helps kids soak up this knowledge. Rachel MacDonald, an elementary school teacher, shared that "there are many things parents can begin to do to ensure their children are successful ... read to them... [and] limit the amount of time their young children spend watching television. Children need to spend more time playing, imagining, pretending, and interacting with others, and less time just sitting and watching."

MacDonald goes on to say, "As they enter into the early grades... successful students know that school is a priority in their home. Parents should make this clear by ensuring their child is on time and in school every day except for illness. Vacations, birthdays, and family visits can be enjoyed on non-school days. Successful students practice skills at home... [and] are responsible. Parents should make sure their children have the books and work that they need for class with them every day. They should also assign chores around the house for their child to give them the opportunity to learn responsibility. Successful students are well-rested... [But] most importantly, polite and respectful of others. Parents need to discuss, encourage, and model good manners, kindness toward others, and the acceptance of others' differences. This will help their child become an excellent student in school and a highly successful adult."

What about those who don't receive that structure at home? As you may have noticed, people spend countless hours on self-improvement—whether it's physically or mentally. They often are not satisfied with who they are, what they look like, or what they are doing with their lives. Middle school and high school students—particularly females ages thirteen to nineteen—especially have difficulties navigating through conflicts and critical decisions in their lives. Imagine the typical high school in the United States with about 750 students. Close to 150 of these students experience bullying at school. Over one-third of the girls and about one-fifth of the boys suffer from some degree of depression.

One hundred seventy students will have been offered or sold drugs and 345 (nearly half) will have had sex. By the end of their senior year, roughly 217 of these students will have dropped out. Does this sound like something your children are experiencing? These are some of the issues youth are facing across the country, and some of the statistics are even grim in Arizona.[1]

Steve Gillett, a school principal, says, "The greatest challenge currently facing American schools is not a weak curriculum or the instructional competencies of teachers; it is meeting the needs of our students before they can begin learning. Not that schools should not share in the responsibility...it is simply that too much of the responsibility has been placed upon the schools. Most schools feed their children breakfast, find ways to work with organizations to clothe those in need, provide before and after school care, and teach drug-awareness education and basic sex-education information. This work goes on while we help children who are hungry, angry, or unmotivated find success in school where standards are of increasingly greater rigor."

Risk Issues for High School Students

In order to help today's youth, we need to be aware of the issues they face that put them at risk. In 2010, about seven thousand high schools students dropped out every day in the US.[2] According to the Alliance for Excellent Education, students who are struggling with grades in their middle school years are likely to become high school dropouts. Childhood obesity, student peer pressure, and bullying add to the risks students face during high school. Donorschoose.org states that "the percentage of overweight children and adolescents in the US has nearly tripled since the early 1970s. More than one in five children between the ages of six and seventeen are now considered overweight. Childhood obesity has been linked to diabetes, high blood pressure, depression, anxiety, and poor academic performance."[3] The percentage of students who experience depression and exposure to drugs and sex is frightening since these behaviors put students at higher risk of disease and dropping out of school. (See the graphics in this chapter and source references at the end of the book to find out more about this research.) "Although fifteen to twenty-four-year-olds represent only one-quarter of the sexually active population, they account for nearly half (9.1 million) of the 18.9 million new cases of STDs each year."[4]

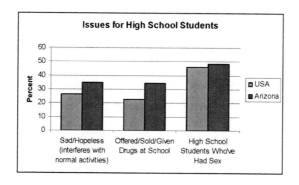

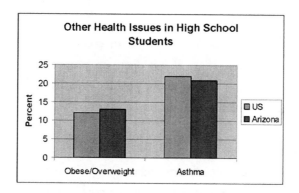

As you know as parents and educators, it is very important that our kids get the best education pertaining to eating right and living a healthy lifestyle. This means exercising and staying fit. Many of us as parents don't encourage our kids to join sporting activities—that is, anything active at all. Some of these kids just sit at home—watching TV, surfing the web, or playing video games. Some opt to sleep or stay lethargic. This is unhealthy and allows youngsters to develop bad habits such as laziness and unproductiveness. To the parents reading this, I would encourage your kids to make healthy eating choices and to implement exercise during their developmental years so that diseases could be avoided in the long run.

Denise Mann, *HealthDay* reporter, stated that "Dr. Yolandra Hancock, a primary care pediatrician at Children's National Medical Center in Washington, D.C., usually stresses the easy-to-understand 5-2-1-0 rule to overweight and obese teens who want and need to lose weight. This refers to five fruits and vegetables a day, two hours or less of screen time such as TV or video games a day, one hour of physical activity a day, and zero or very little sugar-sweetened beverages a day."[5] For those who aren't keen on implementing this rule, compromise is crucial to success. Kids who love to play video games can compromise by using their video games to exercise. Instead of playing sedentary type games, "Just Dance" or games using the "Wii Fit" can be both fun, educational, and help produce results to stay healthy and active.

The bottom line is that we need to combat this issue together, parents and children alike. If we open up proper dialogue, sharing helpful resources and talking about positive experiences, we can begin to tackle these problems head on.

Cancer

Believe it or not, cancer is becoming one of the leading causes of illness in young adults—as my situation can attest to. It's an area that is not widely talked about with youth, so educating others on some of the data proves helpful. Most young people are uneducated about these diseases, therefore feeling like an outcast and unable to relate to their peers. Consider these statistics:

- In the US, cancer is the leading disease that causes death in adolescents.

- Fewer than seventeen percent of children up to nineteen years old have had some form of cancer.
- The most common forms of cancer in children are lymphomas and brain cancers.

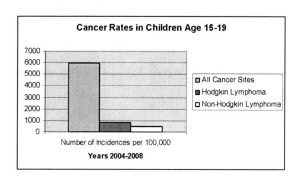

When I was first diagnosed, I had no idea what Hodgkin's was. I didn't posses the tools to help me understand this illness on a larger scale. I had to do my own research and discover what it entailed. When I spoke with my oncology physician, Dr. Robles, he told me Hodgkin's was the most treatable form of cancer. A while after my prognosis, I explored further and found out that my grandfather had passed away from cancer. This disease ran in my family, but I was unaware. That's why I think it's so vital for us as parents and guardians to speak with our kids about our family's health history and talk about potential hereditary effects. Educating our young people on these issues will help them become informed citizens—helping them to strive to take better care of themselves and hopefully, one day, find cures for these diseases.

Bullying

As we touched on in the beginning of this chapter, many young adults are adamant on wanting to change something about their physical appearance. Students might be uncomfortable with their weight; they might think they are abnormal for not looking a certain way. Anything that might be considered insignificant to most can be detrimental and be used as a reason for being bullied. The American Society for the Prevention of Cruelty to Children (ASPCC) shared, "an estimated one hundred sixty thousand students in the USA refuse to go to school because they dread the physical and verbal aggression of their peers. Many more attend school in a chronic state of anxiety and depression. It's reported that six out of ten American youth witness bullying at least once a day. Victims can experience…shame, anxiety, irritability… and depression."[6]

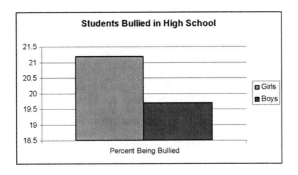

In my work with youth and educators in schools, I explain that there are three types of roles when it comes to bullying: the target, the bystander, and the bully. The target can be a person randomly singled out by any given person or group and put in a position where he or she has to defend himself or herself for any given reason. A bystander can be a friend, classmate, or peer who knows the comrade is being victimized, but for whatever reason, doesn't take the opportunity to stand up for this person. Instead, the bystander watches from the sidelines while the victim is left feeling alone and vulnerable. The bully is the person acting out, thinking he or she is superior over the victim. The bully often preys on a victim's weakness, making that bully feel all the more powerful.

The four types of bullying can be: physical (anything from destroying or stealing a victim's property to actually pushing, shoving, scratching, kicking, slapping, biting, and/or beating someone up). Verbal bullying doesn't leave the marks that physical bullying does, but it can be more damaging and detrimental because of the emotional scars it leaves behind. Social bullying uses relationships to harass someone through gossip, public humiliation, or embarrassment. This tends to be more girl-oriented behavior than boy. Cyber bullying can be tied into social bullying as well. This is a fairly new form of bullying that is spread through the Internet, texting, Facebook, YouTube, and other forms of social media. The victim is often left publicly humiliated; unfortunately, this has resulted in an increase in dropping out of school and even teen suicide.

If your students live in fear of relentless teasing and suffer from self-esteem issues, why would they want to return to the classroom? Why would they want to live? It's important for us as parents to talk with our children about what's going on in their everyday lives. When families are interested and involved, communication is easier, and the child is more likely to open up and talk about the issue. We as parents, teachers, and community members have opportunities and decisions to make when it comes to handling bullying. **We need to let kids know they are valuable and don't have to take maliciousness from others.** The "quirks" that get picked on by bullies can be used as a platform to stand strong. We as mentors can show kids that it's okay to be ODD, meaning that kids can possess **opportunities**, make wise **decisions**, and cultivate **discipline** to help stop this pandemic. When students are empowered to be the "voice" of a victim, they are demonstrating good character qualities that make them effective leaders—thus helping to tear down the strongholds bullying has on our youth.

Teen Pregnancy Rates for Girls Fifteen to Nineteen Years of Age

Another reason it's so vital for parents and other adults to invest in our youth is because of teen pregnancy. If people are not properly educated on options such as abstinence and birth control, things can turn hairy. When parents talk to their kids and show them how to be accountable and responsible for their actions, circumstances will hopefully improve. If wisdom isn't shared, however, consequences can be great.

United States teen pregnancy rates exceed those of many other developed countries. Teen pregnancies cost US taxpayers more than $9 billion per year, and the risks to teen mothers and their children affect everyone.[7]

- Babies born to teen mothers are at higher risk of health problems and infant death.[8]
- Only about 50 percent of teen mothers receive a high school diploma by age twenty-two.
- Lack of education and job skills increase the chance that teen mothers and their children will endure a life of poverty.
- The cycle perpetuates as children of teen mothers tend to have low school achievement and higher school dropout rates and the girls are 33 percent more likely to become teen mothers themselves.

Pregnancy Rates in the US and Arizona

A teen pregnancy rate of over 56 per 1,000 births ranks Arizona much higher than the national level. There

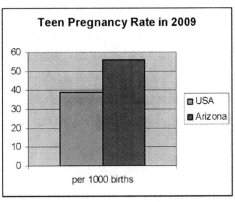

Teen Pregnancy Rate in 2009

were 410,000 teen pregnancies in the US in 2009 and 12,381 of those were in Arizona.

When I look at these statistics, my heart breaks. I don't just see numbers; I see the innocent faces of these young ladies who have been robbed of something vital—love. The influence of a father figure, or lack thereof, might have spurred these young women to search for significance and value. Often, in my opinion, this leads them into sexual exploration prematurely. These young girls get involved with boys who promise them the world, that they'll always be loved and never leave. This is a promise that girls hold onto—the promise to be cherished and adored. The longing they've had since they were little is now being satisfied by the sweet whisperings of hope. However, the "love" these girls experience is really only lies and abandonment cleverly disguised in sheep's clothing. Teen pregnancy and broken hearts are often the end result. When I look at my young daughter, I have to stop and ask myself, *what am I doing as a parent to ensure my little girl feels love?* She doesn't have to seek out attention or security in other ways. She deserves love, and to the best of my ability, I meet that need. Other parents should be doing the same thing—modeling that behavior. That way, when my daughter and others like her grow into adolescence, they will understand and set high standards for themselves and the boys who try to date them. These standards—being secure in self-respect, and protection—help these ladies to ensure and know that love comes about the right way.

High School Dropout Rates

This morning when I woke up, Fox News stated that most schools in the United States have not met the federal standards. For whatever reason, there are many students not interested in learning or attending school. Arizona is ranked thirty-eighth in the nation for graduating high school students in a timely fashion. Thirty-eighth? That's appalling! We as a culture are *losing* the value of family and the positive impact that it can have on our kids. Steve Green, Ph.D., a high school principal, shares that: "Today's high school students are confronted with challenges and pressures unlike those experienced by teens in previous generations. In the classroom, state and national standards have pushed graduation requirements to four years of math and three years of science. Just a few years ago, Arizona's graduating students needed just two credits of each. In their personal lives, social media and other technology have made the world a place focused on the immediate and have exposed teens to the entire world. Yet, teens are still teens, and though they might have more knowledge and awareness, they may not have the emotional support systems necessary to deal with these immediate and potentially dangerous pressures. In the home, the world economy has forced many more teens today to work to help support their families. The family home, because of economic challenges, often does not look like the home of years before. Consequently, teens find it difficult to find the time to study and when they find the time, the atmosphere may not be conducive to study."

For students who drop out of high school, the financial consequences are relatively high. With Arizona's nearly 24,700 students who did not graduate in 2010, the estimated loss of earnings is over $6.4 billion[9], which has a big impact on the economy.

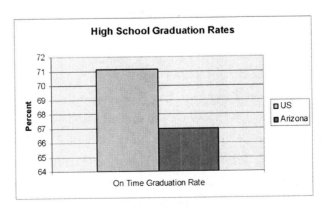

- Nationwide, it is estimated that 1.3 million students dropped out in 2010.
- Students who do not graduate from high school are more likely to have low-income jobs or no jobs at all.
- Crime rates increase with lack of education, as do healthcare and welfare costs.

These issues, coupled with teen pregnancy, can be tied partly to the root of the problem. Most teen mothers do not graduate from high school, therefore taking whatever minimum wage jobs are out there in order to provide for their families. This statistic, when compared to those in Australia and Canada, indicates a more poverty-stricken stance. The other countries reported that even though they have these issues, families are able to better themselves and break the cycle of poverty, whereas in the US and UK, people struggle due to a lack of social mobility.[10] If healthcare and welfare programs were strengthened in the United States, and if teens had access to better abstinence and contraceptive education and higher paying jobs, these statistics might go down and the graduation rate might improve.

In my humble opinion, these statistics indicate a failure on parents' parts. We cannot continue to place blame on schools, faith-based organizations, or community programs. Moms and dads, it's up to us to parent, show our kids love, and teach them discipline and structure. Jamy Beaton shared with me the following thoughts on this, which I think ring true: "It's time parents stopped worrying so much about being their children's friend. Let's get real; they have enough friends. But they only have one mom and one dad. Fellow parents, my message to you is this: We *chose* to create a life. With that comes a responsibility

> Moms and dads, it's up to us to parent, show our kids love, and teach them discipline and structure.

that does not end. Being a parent is 24/7, 365 days, for as long as you live. Period."

Let me ask you: *What kind of example are you setting?*

Call to Action: Your Change Pledge

As part of my *Change: If I Can, You Can* project, I've initiated a Change Pledge for individuals to sign. This is a key part of my events, where I often have youth and attendees come up to sign these commitments as part of my presentation. Please consider writing this pledge on a piece of paper yourself, and signing it as a symbol of your commitment to change:

*I acknowledge myself as a valuable
individual who needs positive change.
I pledge to look within myself and Change for the better.
In doing so, I will strive to help others around me—
while inspiring them, too, to Change for the better.
Change: If I Can, You Can Project.*

*Signed:*_____

CHAPTER 8

IF I CAN, YOU CAN

"What a beautiful morning to thank God and make a difference in someone's life...maybe guiding a kid in the right direction, thanking a soldier in uniform, or sitting down with a senior and being a listening ear. Life is so great—why not make a positive difference in your own life too?"
—Travis Angry

I love people, especially kids, and I love to help and serve alongside them. The choices I made when I was younger, whether wise or foolish, helped shape me into the man I am today. It took a lot of hurdles to get to the place where I feel most productive, but I had to acknowledge my inadequacies and realize there was more to me than that. I realized that some people would judge me by my past, but I couldn't let that past define who I was becoming. Travis Angry was a different man.

If I felt this way, surely others—especially young people—struggled with the same thoughts. How many times have youngsters been told that they are just a bunch of hoodlums, out to cause trouble and raise ruckus? Often when an older person sees a teenager, his or her mind immediately goes to the negative. When kids act up or act out, no one takes the time to understand why they are this way. All kinds of assumptions are made, but no one bothers to ask or understand that perhaps that child's home life isn't pleasant or safe. Absentee parenting is in full swing, as are druggie parents who don't give a rat's ass about their kids; verbal and physical abuse are rampant. There are struggles of students being the primary caretakers of their siblings while their single mother works two jobs just to put food on the table. A father cheats on his wife and abandons the family, leaving behind heartache that needs understanding. No one expresses interest in these young peoples' lives, so they don't speak up either. Because of this, they are seen as nothing but apathetic teenagers or unruly kids who only run amuck.

What adults fail to realize is that these kids crave attention. They're acting out primarily because love isn't prevalent in their lives. Most kids think that if their parents don't show any interest in them, they need to find someone who will. Young kids and teenagers long to be noticed, valued, and loved. If parents don't care, why should kids? Steve Schembri, my dear friend, shares, "There is an old cliché that kids are like sponges—and it's true. Kids soak up everything around them. Here is a simple test to prove my statement: Tune the radio to your children's favorite song, or turn on their favorite movie; then listen as they recite the lyrics and mimic the main character's actions. This idea that kids feast on their environment extends beyond the media; however. They absorb what you do. *Fathers—they internalize how you treat your wives. Mothers—they hear what you say to your girlfriend on the phone while you drive them to practice.* Kids hear, see, and more importantly, feed on everything you do and say—good and bad." With this realization, one must see how

Fathers—they internalize how you treat your wives. Mothers—they hear what you say to your girlfriend on the phone while you drive them to practice.

vital it is to invest positively in
these young people.

ShaRon Rea, author and
founder of *The Whole Family*,
also has a consistent message
she shared with me: "Positive
Family Relationships Begin
With You™. Parents are the
leaders of the family, and our children need us to lead responsibly,
with strong convictions and unconditional love. We can change the
direction of this dysfunctional path our youth are on and support them
as they create a future where they will thrive and truly be proud of who
they are."

There was a sermon series at my church regarding family, focused
on the dynamic of parenting. The pastor challenged us that if we wanted
to know how lost our youth culture had become, to head to the mall,
sit, and observe our surroundings for an hour. I was amazed at what
I witnessed. One girl, who appeared to be around fourteen years old,
stood in front of Bakers shoe store with her mom. She told her mother
that she wanted a particular type of shoe, but for whatever reason, her
mother told her no. This young girl threatened her mom and said, "You
better buy me these shoes or else!" The mother did nothing—she didn't
reprimand her daughter or anything.

A little while later, I witnessed a similar situation. A young man,
about sixteen, was in an athletic store with his father. The teenager
wanted a particular kind of shoe, but his dad told him he couldn't get
it. The kid got so upset over his dad's refusal that he ended up punching
his father in the face! Mall security had to come and break up the fight!
I share these stories because, as an observer, these parents didn't seem to
possess control. There was a lack of discipline, and the teen's behavior
exhibited that. These scenarios made me think back to a time when I
was about twelve years old and went shopping with my mother at Foot

Locker. This kid in the store whined about getting his own way and his mother gave in and bought him some very expensive tennis shoes. When he left the store, I decided that I would try it on my mom. I told her I wanted to get some pricey Air Jordan sneakers. She told me that I couldn't get them because they were too expensive. I started to whine in hopes of getting my mom to cave.

WHACK! My mother had slapped me across my cheek. Whether you agree with spanking or not, that was her way of telling me that she had already given me her answer and that was final. When we got to the car, she laid into me about respecting her and not making a spectacle in public. I learned my lesson and realized I wasn't to test my mother's authority. My mother had set the standard that day.

My mother and father took the time and laid the foundation of love in their own way—through good parenting and discipline. Though affection was not a leading quality in my family, my folks truly understood the importance of being a parent. The values and morals they instilled in me have helped me to become a better man and father of two amazing kids. The standards they set also gave me a strong foundation for success. They taught me that having a plan of action was key, and to do everything to the best of my ability. We weren't the perfect family by any means, but these qualities helped to ensure a strong household.

Parents and guardians, we must realize that children are like flowers; needing to be cared for, nurtured, and watered so they can blossom into something spectacular. We need to realize we've been given a monumental and awesome task of cultivating these youth. During their developmental stages, it is crucial that we show kids love and teach them respect—that we as adults are in charge—and instill in them the difference between right and wrong. We need to give these kiddos a strong foundation, and teach them responsibility and drive. Don't wait until your child is already grown to "water" him or her.

Our youth should focus on becoming the best individuals they can. We need to show them that behavior can dictate outcome. When they utilize the firm foundation their parents have laid, they are likely to have a more positive mind-set and focus on their full potential. Making the right decisions and having the right priorities make for a positive life. However, if this isn't being modeled, the talents they have can be wasted. The biggest red flag I see in our society is that parents try to be the friend first and then the parent. They let their kids get away with talking to them on their level—often not correcting their negative attitudes or disrespectful behavior. Or, it goes the other way. Parents who have successful kids hone in on their talents and "ride" them to the point of perfection. This happens in many areas—like sports, cheerleading, singing, academics, acting, and writing, just to name a few. However, these young kids need to understand that they will never make it on talent alone, and parents need to reinforce that reality. *Discipline and drive is their key to success!* Without these key ingredients, their talents will diminish. We can see it every day in professional athletics—some talented athletes make poor decisions that cost their team a win or a championship. Look at football players who get a fifteen yard penalty for unsportsmanlike conduct. They don't exhibit self-control; why? Because they lack discipline. Look at the singer Chris Brown, an amazingly talented, young singer who almost lost everything when he assaulted his girlfriend, Rihanna. *Why? Because of lack of discipline.* These situations make me look at the parents of these celebrities and wonder how they raised their kids. Was there discipline or a strong foundation set for success?

Chelsea Jarvis, an elementary school teacher, said "I wish…we could get all the parents into one room and give them a wakeup call of what is happening with their children. We can make a difference in these kids' lives… show them it is possible to have dreams and achieve success in their life." Our youth culture should be able to dream freely and get excited about their future. They should have access to role-models who will spur them on to make wise decisions when it comes to their own lives. When young people hear the personal stories of others who've endured hardships and overcame them, it is more likely to resonate in them becoming better themselves. For example, the story of my good friend, Tom Still, as told by his parents, David and Esther Still, is one of "beating all odds." They shared this story with me:

The Tom Still Story

"When our son Tom was in the middle of his F-16 training for the US Air Force, he had a devastating experience. He had been going through flight training for 1.5 years with his wings in T-37 and T-38 trainer aircraft. He had his glider and single engine propeller wings also. It was the fall of 2002, and in the last three months of F-16 training, he went to his flight surgeon because of a cough, some discomfort in his chest, and numbness in his right hand. He was sent for an x-ray and then immediately for a CAT scan. The results showed a large tumor the size of a grapefruit in the right side of his chest which turned out to be Non-Hodgkin's Lymphoma. Tom had been a good athlete and had never really been sick in his life. He was fortunate to graduate from the US Air Force Academy in Colorado Springs with academic honors and athletic distinction.

After some medical visits in Arizona where he was going through training, the Air Force agreed to let Tom come back to Seattle, his home base, for treatment. We were fortunate to get into the Seattle Cancer Care Alliance and had a wonderful doctor/oncologist, Dr. Gopal. It was determined that Tom would need eight rounds of chemo and then radiation. In February of 2003, after the sixth treatment, a PET scan showed that the cancer was gone; thus the last two treatments were not necessary. But the twenty-plus radiation treatments were still ahead of him.

During all of this, our son demonstrated a positive attitude and did things like help out with a junior high basketball team, lead a Bible study, and help out with a local Young Life group. In January 2003 when he was still going through chemotherapy, he went to Arizona to see his F-16 class graduate. After completing the radiation, he returned to Arizona to do a desk job at the base. A year later, the medical board for the Air Force decided to put Tom through a battery of tests, which showed he could physically go back to flying. He received a medial waiver to fly. Tom started his F-16 training all over again and graduated in May the following year. That was one special occasion and we all felt so blessed that God gave him this second chance. Tom is still flying that plane and loving it! He completed his third war tour, flying more than one hundred combat missions, and has received four flying medals."

This is truly a remarkable story. Tom was a man who was minding his own business, concentrating on what he loved to do, and then life threw him a curve ball. He could have sulked and went into a downward spiral, but he pulled himself up by his bootstraps and persevered. Like Tom, when I served in the military, I had my own battles I fought. There were good days and dark days, but one thing was for certain: We had to keep moving forward. Robert Frost once said that life can be summed up into three words, "It goes on." That statement is certainly true. Even though life got difficult, I didn't have to go at it alone. I had people come alongside to encourage me and help me through, thus helping me instill confidence in myself that things can get better.

I can't stress it enough: Young people *need* encouragement and motivation to become the best they can be. However, in order for youngsters to understand the importance of becoming a great leader, they need to know what it's like to be a follower. For example, when I served in the military, boot camp taught me how to do and be the best. When it was time to go to battle in Iraq, I was able to implement what I had learned to make my mission successful.

My parents were both educators in the Dade County Public School System in Florida; my father was a teacher and principal for thirty-seven years, and my mother for twenty. They used to tell me stories about how previous generations tossed aside core values that their forefathers fought so hard to achieve. They would equate the rest of the world the same way—how the lack of discipline resulted in the same behavior—often manifesting in crime, disrespect for fellow man, and war. In the same way, today's students exhibit the good, the bad, and the ugly. Some lack leadership, parenting, or having their basic needs met. They disrespect authority figures and live a wayward life. However, some students in dire straits still manage to graduate, go to college, and make a difference.

Young people, setting goals is another important part of life that ensures success. My father used to say that if you don't have goals to reach for, you will never move in life. Setting short and long-term goals will help motivate you to get to the next milestone in your desired area of life. Here are some key things that helped me figure out my plan of attack and make practical steps toward positive change in life. (Feel free to alter them as you see fit.)

1. **Talk to a pastor or other trusted adults about getting your life on track.** The Bible has a lot of examples of people who have been through some tough challenges and how they overcame. Consider reading the book of John, or the book of Proverbs that talks about applying wisdom to everyday life.

2. **Take time every day to clear your head and take an honest analysis of where you are mentally, emotionally, and physically.** Have an honest dialogue with yourself (and God). Freely express the emotions you are experiencing and ask (God) for clarity. Ask yourself how you can be a better you. No one else can take stalk of your own life like you can. You owe it to yourself.

3. **Reconcile broken relationships.** Extend forgiveness and ask forgiveness. It's not an easy feat, but does produce healing.

4. **Hang out with those who can build you up.** Seek help from someone you trust to help deal with issues. Consider getting connected to a small group through a local church with people who can encourage you to cultivate your strengths. Be careful who you hang out with, because they can rub off on you— choose your friends wisely!

5. **Identify the road blocks that keep you from making changes in your life.** Is it negative thinking, a poor self-image, or confidence issues? Make a list of what your limitations are, but list them as positive statements. Then, set goals or steps change those negatives into positives.

The greatest leaders are the ones who understand humility, compromise, and how to be team players. If you have drive and determination, doors of opportunity will open up for you to be triumphant whatever the task. My opportunity came when I met presidential candidate Herman Cain. Our stories paralleled, and I told him I wanted to be the first African-American senator from the state of Arizona. He looked me in the eye and reaffirmed my call to action. Discover the value of being a follower—learn from those who motivate and cultivate the qualities that matter. Like Herman Cain suggests in his book, *This is Herman Cain*, become the CEO of your own life. Find a mentor (like I did with Herman Cain) who can identify and/or parallel with your story, and glean from this person all the insight you can and reaffirm your belief in yourself.

Then, look outwardly and see how you can become an activist of positive change in the world around you. Understand this isn't just happening on US soil; the entire world is being affected by poverty and abuse. While on tour in Iraq, I witnessed firsthand the exploitation of innocent people—children being mistreated, women being beaten, fathers fighting an unsettling war. They were broken and hurting, needing someone to give them a glimmer of hope that things could improve. Be the person who stands up for freedom and justice. We need an international movement that addresses these world issues. We need to educate others and provide the tools of what a strong foundation looks like. We need to mend families. We need others to understand that when babies are brought into this world, they have a fighting chance. Be part of the *Change: If I Can, You Can movement* so kids around the world have a chance at a bright future.

Parents, guardians, teachers, please hear my heart when I say this: Your kids *need* you. Your presence and example is so vital. Our youth need your encouragement, your voice, and your support. They need you to be strong when they are weak, firm when they want to break the rules and a soft place to land when they fall. *They need you.* If you want to make a significant impact on a young person's life, simply show up, be a person of noble character, and be available. Allow these kids to see you interested and invested in their lives,

> Parents, guardians, teachers, please hear my heart when I say this: Your kids *need* you.

regardless of the choices they've made. Help those kids facing negative situations turn their circumstances into positives. If you see a teen mom, walk alongside her and show her she can make a difference in the life of her baby. If someone is struggling at home, give him or her an outlet to vent. If you know those who are struggling at school, encourage them to keep up with their studies and pursue their degree. Most of all, *believe* in them. When young people see you caring and supportive, it will instill hope in them to succeed. Be part of the movement and help our youth culture attain positive change. Remember, ***Change: If I Can, You Can...*** Let's get started! Note: To find out how to join the movement, visit my website and connect with me: www.TravisAngry.com.

EPILOGUE

The Bible says in Matthew 6:34, *"Don't worry about missing out. You'll find your everyday human concerns will be met. Give your entire attention to what God is doing right now, and don't get worked up about what may or may not happen tomorrow. God will help you deal with whatever hard things come up when the time comes."*

Hear those words: ...**help you deal**...? Those are the words that resonate in my being when I think about the movement of ***Change: If I Can, You Can.*** With every passionate breath within me, my desire is to have young people see and understand that obstacles are a part of life. **They are inevitable.** *The question is: What am I going to do about it? How am I going to handle this?*

You've read my story. You, dear reader and friend, have now become part of my story—part of my journey. You have been a spectator on the sidelines of my life and witnessed my reaction to life's dealings. Once again, I've had to get in the ring with life. I was an average Joe—an underdog, targeted multiple times by the bullies of life: from not fitting in, to enduring family issues, to the heartache of rejection that came from divorce, to the challenges of single fatherhood. Throughout many of those stages, I was targeted by an even bigger bully who shadowed my path and threatened to steal my life: cancer.

That ugly, nasty, no good thug, Hodgkin's Lymphoma, reared its ugly head again in my life in 2011 and 2012. In fact, I had to undergo six months of chemotherapy while being a single dad—which was no small feat. I had a choice to make: Was I going to back down to this cancer and let it take over…or was I going to stand up and fight?

I made a decision. I wasn't going to be afraid. When I felt lonely and overwhelmed and struggled for that next measure of strength, I grasped for it. I didn't know what the next day was going to bring but I heard those words…*help you deal.* When those hard moments of vomiting and medicinal drips coursed through my veins, I remember I had *a choice* of how I was going to react. Sure, there were moments I cried. I felt afraid, I worried, even stressed. I felt those human emotions. Was I going to die? *Change…*

No, I wasn't going to let cancer beat me. I was going to fight for my life, moment by moment, day by day. I was going to persevere with the help and encouragement of God, and the strength of my parents' spirits— for my children—and I was going to succeed because of all of you. *You, dear reader, were my momentum. You were my inspiration to keep tacklin'…to keep battlin'.* My mission to reach the hearts and lives of youth and adults worldwide has kept me fighting for life, and for a positive outcome in all I do.

After a long, hard, treacherous battle, I am proud to say that I am ending 2012 on a higher note than when it began. I can once again say, proudly and boldly, I am a TWO TIME cancer survivor! I have fought with everything I've had, struggled to achieve my dream, faced insurmountable obstacles and wanderings in the desert, and still, I am like a Phoenix…I have arisen again. And so, this message rings stronger than ever:

Change: If I Can, You Can.

APPENDIX

First Motivational Speech Ever Given by Travis Angry

I've included this speech *transcript as a way of documenting the beginning of my journey in being a motivational speaker. This is the slightly edited transcript of the very first speech I ever gave—at my college graduation day luncheon on November 11, 2011, to a group of family, friends, and colleagues. The speeches I give today to schools and other groups touch on some of these same themes, although the topics have adapted to include additional motivational concepts (for more on my speeches, see www. TravisAngry.com):*

Today is a new beginning of a new journey in my life, and before I begin, I would like to say thank you to every single person in this room. Every single person in this room has played a very integral part in my life.

I wanted to do this event today because I wanted to give back. Sometimes in life, we are on the receiving end, and we fail to remember about giving back. Family and friends, this is my opportunity to say thank you from the bottom of my heart.

The *CHANGE: If I Can, You Can* project started about six years ago when I was going through chemotherapy at the VA hospital. Doing this

153

treatment, I had the opportunity to do a lot of reflection on where I started and where I am today. I came to the conclusion that I wanted to make a difference. I did not want to sit on the sidelines anymore.

Today's youth are in a crisis. Our teens feel so much hurt, so much pain. They lack guidance. They have no respect for their parents or authority. I was this young man—who did not have that respect. The challenges that our youth culture face today are similar challenges that I went through.

We have a big challenge. We're going up against cell phones. We're going up against the Internet. We're going up against TV. We have a big challenge, moms and dads, and this challenge is in our own homes. Dr. Gary Chapman, the author of the book that I've been reading the last couple days, talks about the value of a parent in our teen's life. He goes on to say that statistics show that parents have the most effect on a kid's life.

I dropped out of school back in January of 1992. I'm never going to forget that day when I made that decision. I made that decision to just give up on life, give up on education. Expectations were high. I was very jealous of my older brother. Like Jennifer Wright said, I felt as though I was a victim; I blamed everyone for my problems, and finally I had to look in the mirror and say, *You know what? You create your own destiny. God gives you the life to say yes or no.* But most importantly, I had two parents who really believed in me. I had two parents who really, truly loved me unconditionally. I put my parents through a lot back in 1992. I broke my dad's heart. You have to understand, my dad had been teaching in a school system for almost twenty-five years at the time, and, to have a son give up on education, broke his heart.

Most importantly, as I do my reflection, I started to do some research. You see, when I started the *CHANGE: If I Can You Can* project, it's not something that I just took on and said, "You know what; I think I'm going to do it." I did a lot of research, and I looked at our teens. And when I came to Arizona, I fell in love with the desert. I love this state, and I just don't see myself moving. I tell a lot of people that I see myself retiring somewhere in a rural area—up in Prescott or Flagstaff because I love this state. But when I look at what our kids are doing within this state when it comes to high school graduate rates—71 percent are on time in the United States. Arizona is right behind the national rate at 67 percent on time in Arizona.

In 2010, 24,700 dropouts occurred in Arizona. Arizona is thirty-eighth in the nation for graduating high school students on time. We can do better. I can talk about this because I dropped out. You see, sometimes when you talk about something, if you have the experience, that experience gives you the knowledge, gives you the wisdom to say, "You know what? I was that dropout." I was that young man who said, "You know what? I can't be a college graduate. I can't graduate from school. Me, Travis Angry, a college graduate?" It was something that I could never even allow myself to think back in 1992.

The cost of dropping out is significant. It's not just significant in our homes, but it's significant in our communities. What is the impact of our dropouts? Lower-income jobs, increase in crime rates, increase to taxpayers in health care and welfare costs. It's estimated that in Arizona, 6.4 billion in lost earnings is due to dropouts. Is the value of higher learning going backwards? Or is it something that needs to be enforced and encouraged in going forward? Kids not only have the issue with dropouts, but there are other issues that they deal with on a consistent basis: peer pressure, bullying, and an increase in childhood obesity. That is the one that really shocked me the most when I did the research. I didn't realize that childhood obesity was so serious until I really delved into the research of it. Getting involved in drugs and other risky behaviors, depression, suicide—the list goes on and on.

But it's not just dropouts that our kids are struggling with. It's also the disease that I struggled with back in 2005: cancer. Cancer is the leading disease causing death in adolescents. Nearly 17 percent of children up to nineteen years old have cancer. Most common lymphomas and brain cancers are in our adolescents. This is devastating financially and emotionally. Cancers and other diseases affect everyone. Again, the cost is huge financially and emotionally.

Where does Travis Angry come in to play? Well, I decided I was going to incorporate. I incorporated my company: Travis Angry Incorporated. Our organizational mission, is very clear; it's very concise: *We're here to impact our youth culture for positive change.* No longer will we sit on the sidelines and allow our kids to go down the wrong path that I went down and through. Instead, we aim to inspire—to empower our teens to think, feel, and dream about ways to create a positive change in their lives and make correct choices for a better future. They deserve that, we need to give that to them, and I want to be the leader in letting them know: *We believe in you.*

I aim to create a coalition of youths to commit to change within and then inspire change around them. I want them to understand that they can change, but the value is not just in changing, but is also in doing what the military does while on a mission. We're always trying to figure out what can we do to help the soldier, sailor, airman, and Marine. I want kids to inspire each other, create an inspiration among them, where they can tell each other, *Change: If I Can, You Can.* I want to encourage participation in a national youth movement leading teens to become great citizens and to help improve the lives of people in the surrounding communities. **When they succeed at home, the community succeeds. When the community succeeds, then the city succeeds. It's a ripple effect that goes all the way up to our national level.**

This is where Travis Angry Inc. comes in. we're not here to force change; we're here to inspire. You guys see my business cards on your tables. If you look on the back, it says *youth inspirational motivational speaker.* The inspirational component is to inspire our youth based upon my story and based upon my example. The motivational component is to motivate the parents to get into their kids' lives. It's a winning combination from child to parent. When this wins, these rates go down.

That is the objectives. So many parents are sitting on the sidelines and some parents need to get off the sidelines and get into the game of their kid's life.

A player might tell his coach: "Coach, let me get in! I want to play! Or moms might say: "I want to get in my daughter's life. I have not been that good role model. I want to be in her life and let her know what it's like to show respect to your body. I've been out of my daughter's life for so long, she needs me; let me get in!"

When I look at my daughter, I want her to understand that her dad believes in her. I want to give her the security. I want to inspire her. I want to give her everything she knows so that when she gets older she realizes the value, not only of her body, but also what love is about.

Today's teen girls are dealing with so much in their lives. And, they need us at the very biggest points in their lives. Why? Bringing a child into this world is a responsibility; it's a responsibility that some people take lightly. And when I see teen moms, I get so sad when I don't see the support system; as we really motivate a mother, as we really inspire her, as we really walk with her, as we really guide her—when she succeeds, so does the baby inside her. That baby now has the opportunity to succeed. We're creating a ripple effect for positive change, not just turning our backs on this young girl at the most important time in her life, but letting her know that we believe in her.

Everyone makes mistakes. I've made mistakes. I dropped out of school. I had a very, very bad relationship with my father. My father and I fought all the time, and I always blamed him for my mistakes. But as I look back on life at those most important times that I needed him, he was always there. Dr. Angry was always there. He believed in me. He prayed with me. He guided me. He was that example. He showed me what it was like to love a woman—what it is like to honor a woman. What it is like to step up to a woman and say, "I'm wrong," and that you want to get better. My parents showed me and my brothers forty-two years of a beautiful marriage. If you want to win in life, if you want to give your kids the gift so they can see, a beautiful marriage is the best gift, the best ingredient. The next best ingredient is being that role model; there is value in being that.

I drifted in my life. I had low self-esteem. I got into gangs because I wanted attention. I wanted to hang around crowds because I wanted attention. I was willing to do whatever I needed to do to make someone look at me, make someone want to be a part of me—want to be a part of the gang.

You know, back in 2008, I really hit the lowest part of my life when my marriage ended. This is tough because I really believe in the Bible. I believe in the Bible with all of my heart. But God has given me a challenge. Like my doctors said, I have really been through a lot. But people always ask me, "Travis, why are you so happy? Why are you so happy?" Because when you've been through what I've been through and see what God has done for me, there is one word that defines me, and there's one word that I love so much, and there's one word I'm going to take to my grave, and that is *grace*. Grace is what saved me. Grace is what brought me through this tough storm. Grace is what's going to lead me to where I need to go because this world is not my home. I'm only passing through for he has something greater in store for me. Something that I want and something you should want, too.

CHANGE: If I Can, You Can. This movement begins now. If you want to be a part of this movement, get off the sidelines, get into your kids' lives, be that difference. Don't rely on faith-based organizations to do the work for you, or at least all of it. Don't rely on schools to do all of it for you. Don't rely on after school programs to do it for you. Be that leading force in your kids' lives, because right now, they don't have any discipline.

We're celebrating Veteran's Day weekend, and I've seen some kids show no respect whatsoever towards our veterans. That's appalling to me. That type of service and display of discipline should be of value. Discipline is so valuable to success. **A life without discipline is a life**

without success. *In order to be successful in this life, there has to be a foundation of discipline. Discipline takes you higher. Discipline can open up doors. Discipline can open up that job that you've been wanting, but discipline lets you have the best love in the world, and that's your faith.* And to all youngsters in this room, if I was to give you one piece of advice that you could take with you: Lean on your faith. Number two: Love your mom and dad. *Love your mom and dad.* If you can love your mom and dad and respect them with all dignity, you can walk out these doors and be successful.

So many kids are disrespectful to their parents, and they're going backwards. As parents, do you want to be successful in your kid's life? Do what my father and mother did for me, and *let me go. Let me fall. Let me fall.* What's the result of that? I got back up and I became somebody. I am the man I am today because of my parents. My parents gave me the standard. That's why today I can call myself a college graduate, which is something that I never thought about. But as I was sitting in the University of Phoenix Stadium today, I said to myself the big winners today are my kids. They are the winners. Why? Because they have a father who has stepped up to the plate and given them the standards. There is value in giving your kids the standards that they need to meet. So many kids don't have any goals to reach for because there are no standards; there are no standards in the home to reach for. My kids have the standard.

Never tell me I can't do something. That's the biggest no-no. You don't want to tell Travis Angry he can't do it. That sounded so good, I want to say it again: *You do not tell Travis Angry he cannot do it, because through grace I'm going to find a way. Through grace, I will find a way.*

It feels so good to be up here. *I'm actually doing this.* Doesn't it feel great to make a difference in someone's life? Doesn't it feel great to talk to youngsters and tell them what it is that you can do—your story?

In 2010, I had to make a tough decision. My kids needed me, and I'm not going to go into too much depth, but I'm giving you a scenario.

They needed me; they needed a father to step up to the plate. They were in a situation where their environment was not healthy. And, I had to look and say to myself, *Okay, my kids are going into a very unhealthy environment—and I'm living in a beautiful, three bedroom, two bathroom home in south Phoenix.* As I was reflecting on my life, I said to myself, *Look at what God has done for me. Yeah single life is good.*

But my kids needed me. So I said to myself, *I'm going to get off the sidelines, and I'm going to fly up to Michigan, purchase a roundtrip ticket, purchase two more one-way tickets, and I'm going to bring my kids here. I'm going raise my daughter and son to be a woman of standards and a young man of honor.* That is so valuable to me. God gives us the best gifts in the world. Besides life, he gives us our kids. My kids needed me, and I gave up all of that for them. I had so many people, including Doc Angry… Here's how the conversation with my dad went:

Travis: *Hey, Dad. I'm going up to Michigan to get my kids.*

Dr. Angry: *Okay, when you taking em' back?*

Travis: *I'm not.*

Dr. Angry: *Well, what do you mean?*

Travis: *I'm going to raise em'.*

Dr. Angry: *Travis, c'mon; who you fooling?*

Travis: *Dad, you and Mom gave me forty-two years of a beautiful marriage, and I'm going to continue that legacy, and I'm going to make you proud, and I'm going to go get my kids. Is it going to be a challenge? Absolutely. Am I going to fall down? Absolutely. Am I going to be the perfect parent? No, I'm not; but I'm going to do everything I can to honor your legacy.*

He could do nothing but respect that. Then, when I succeeded in doing it, before he passed away, he called me up and said, "Travis, I'm proud of you. Your mother would be so proud of you. You are raising our grandkids so well."

And that's what I try to do. I'm not the perfect parent. But when people told me I couldn't do it, I didn't listen. They said: "You can't be a full-time dad. There's no way in the world you can do it." But I did it. You can talk to my babysitter; she'll let you know. I'm on point. I don't play around when it comes to my kids. I am a loving father, but I am a disciplinarian. Why? Because my grandfather told me, "When I went to church one time, I made the mistake of cursing at church." My family is from Georgia, so you have to understand, this is a Southern thing. He looked at me and says, "If I didn't love you, I wouldn't discipline you. *If I did not love you, I would not discipline you.*" You love your kids? You give them the discipline.

One of the greatest moments that I've had in my life besides having my kids and besides giving my life to Christ is when I went to serve with about five thousand sailors and Marines, and I went to Iraq. We went through the Straits of Hormuz, which is one of the most dangerous— Lt. Commander Farberry can tell you this—one of the most dangerous spots in the whole wide world. You have Iran on one side, Saudi on one side, you got ships coming in, and I'm not going to lie to you, it was one of the most terrifying experiences I've ever had. It is a pleasure to call myself a veteran. It is a pleasure to know that I served with great men for the past, present, and future. It is also great to know that I can call myself a college graduate. That's great; that deserves a round of applause. I've been waiting for when I was going to get my first round of applause!

But before I go any further, I think it's time for me to introduce three of the most amazing men in America: my three brothers. They've come all the way from Florida and New York. People who know me know this: I've been crying about my family to come to Arizona. They're here. When did I know my brothers were actually in Arizona? When we all got in the car and they started picking on me. I was like, *Okay, we're back to normal.* It's like wow; but they're here, and I want to introduce them.

[Travis introduced his brothers starting with his older brother, the musician. He then introduced his brother, the comedian. Lastly, he introduced his youngest brother, who had been the caretaker for both of his parents. He then introduced his children.]

Friends, I did not accept the status quo. I still refuse to accept the status quo. I refuse to accept that we're just going to let these statistics stay where they are. We have to do better. Our kids need us. You need them. Our country needs them, and we all need to do whatever we can to make a difference

Travisangry.com, is waiting for you. You're a parent, right? You have the best opportunity to make a difference in your kid's life, and you're my solution. I want to walk with you, and I want to motivate you to help me help yourself. Because when you win as a parent, so do your kids.

Excuses don't solve issues. Excuses hold up the process. As parents, we need to say, "I'm here to walk with you, not do it for you." Teachers are educators; teachers are not parents. Did everyone hear that? *Teachers are educators; teachers are not parents.* When I look at my kids, I say to myself, *I'm going to be that parent.* I also have the wish factor. We have a wish factor.

I'm sorry, I'm having a come to Jesus moment, but I've gotta give it to you real. I challenge the principal who is sitting right there to call me up and tell me my daughter has disrespected her teacher. Oh Lord no; oh no. That's not acceptable. Why? Because my daughter is not on the same level as her teacher.

The biggest problem is that these kids talk as though they are on the same level as their teachers. Is there any wonder why these numbers are the way they are? So when I look at my daughter, in order for her to be successful in the classroom, I have to parent. I have to let her understand that she will go to school, and she is going to learn. And when she's successful in learning, she's successful in the community, period.

That is my objective. My objective is to let Steve and his entire staff educate, not parent. And that is what I do with my daughter and my son, and they're so obedient. As a parent, the biggest gift you get is when someone tells you your kids are so well-behaved. Why? Because you know you're doing well.

So my conclusion is this: *You're my solution.* My other solution is yes, I do want to walk with your kids. Yes, I want to create a forum so they can walk in and express themselves and feel as though they can succeed. Hear my story: Yes, I dropped out of school. *You can complete your degree.* Hear my story: Yes, I went through cancer. *Yes, I know you're at stage three, but God has a plan for you. He didn't give up on me and he's definitely not going to give up on you.* Just believe in yourself, and you will succeed. Yes, I had a bad relationship with my father, but we overcame that. When I first went through chemotherapy, the first person who walked in shocked me. My dad walked in. I couldn't believe it; I was shocked because we had just been fighting the other day, but he walked in. He walked in with his Bible. Okay, let's go. He threw the Bible on the table, and said, "Let's take this cancer, and let's take it back." And he prayed with me, and he talked with me, and he gave me the best gift in the world when he told me he was proud of me. Man, for my father to tell me that he is proud of me was significant, and it's something I continue to hold in my heart to this day.

Dr. Angry was one of the most amazing men I've ever known, and to call him my father is amazing. Have you really heard this speech? Did you hear my parents mentioned multiple times in my speech? Did everyone get that? You see how important it is when parents are there? You see?

I challenge you all to help me as I move forward with this company. Opportunities are coming. I've just been offered a major contract out of New York City. A major public relations firm has offered me a major, major, major contract. My attorneys are overlooking the contract right now that's going to have me on the top forty radio stations all over this country. They heard about my story; they went onto my website. Right now, I can tell you this website is making a difference. If you have not gone onto it, I've told my story and I'm going to continue to tell my story. I'm writing my book right now: *CHANGE: If I Can, You Can.* If I can go through all of this, why can't you? If I can succeed through this, why can't you? Excuses hold us up; excuses do not bring us far.

I want to give a tribute to my parents ... I just lost my parents within the last year. We lost Mom last year (July); I lost dad this year. I was sitting in the stadium thinking, *I wonder what my dad would be telling me now; I wonder what my mother would be telling me right now.* Well, my mother wouldn't be telling me too much because she was not a woman who had a lot of words. She was very quiet, very graceful. She would just be saying, "Okay, he gets it."

My dad on the other hand; oh my dad was such a character. My dad would say, "That's my boy..."

There is value is saying *that's my son.* There's value in saying *that's my daughter.* My parents are two of the most magnificent people, and the tribute to them is their story. My dad had a hard time after the Vietnam War. He had a hard time losing my grandmother. He had a hard time, but he showed me what change is all about. Yeah, he went through alcoholism. Yeah, he went through struggles the first couple years of his marriage; but one thing I can tell you right now, and my brothers can tell you, is this: he loved his wife. Nothing came between my dad and his wife.

I remember countless times when I used to tell my parents, "You love Mommy more than you love me."

And he was like, "Yes, I do. That's my wife, and you'll understand what I'm saying when you get married."

He did everything he could to be that good example. He worked two or three jobs at one point when my mom was a stay-at-home mom. Two to three jobs, four boys. That's amazing. He went on to become a minister. I get my speaking abilities from my dad. All of this is from my dad. In between him is God. I know God has given me a talent.

My dad was teaching in the school system for more than thirty-six years when he went through his battle with colon cancer; he had to stop working and had a hard time. Why? Because he was so used to going to work every single day. He would tell my brothers and me all the time, "Whatever job you have—it doesn't matter what you do. It doesn't matter if you rake leaves or cut grass or if you're a janitor. It doesn't matter what you do; do it to the best of your abilities." He went on to become a doctor. He got a Ph.D. in education. He went on to be a professor in Ft. Lauderdale.

My mother is from the Bahamas; she came over to the United States and didn't speak proper English. She had to learn how to speak proper English. I saw my dad work with my mother every single day in helping her get her education. She went and got her G.E.D. My dad said, "You know what? You're going to get your bachelor's." He helped her again; she got her bachelor's degree. This is a woman coming from the Bahamian Islands who hadn't been to school for years. She got her bachelor's and went and got her master's.

She was in the hospital, and she had a laptop, and she was working on her Ph.D. She worked on it until she couldn't do anything anymore—amazing. She worked on her Ph.D., and right after she passed away, I got a call from my dad—my dad was crying and he said, "University just awarded your mom her Ph.D." Wow, talk about setting the standard; that's what it's all about.

As I end this, to live on in their legacy and give my kids that same gift, I promise myself one thing within the next four or five years: *One day, I will be known as Dr. Travis Angry.*

ABOUT THE AUTHORS

 **Travis Angry**, youth inspirational-motivational speaker, military veteran, and two-time cancer survivor, received his Bachelor of Science degree in Business and Public Administration and launched his inspirational youth outreach project, *Change: If I Can, You Can,* in November 2011. Travis's vision for *Change: If I Can, You Can* serves as a catalyst to give youth resources and life-long connections to help them deal with their difficulties and make positive life choices. His story of optimism and hope will be shared at youth conferences, speaking engagements, churches, schools, and various other outlets such as *Change: If I Can, You Can* Youth Conference and Dinner Gala 2014. Travis resides in Peoria, Arizona, as a single father with his two children, Tatiyana and DeVante.

Visit www.TravisAngry.com

Wendie Davis-Grauer holds a Bachelor's degree in Secondary Education/English and has been a professional, freelance writer since 2003. She served as a contributing writer for six years to the *Arizona Family News*, a faith-based monthly publication. Wendie continues to hone her skills in various areas of the writing field such as ghostwriting, aviation, and interviewing. Wendie is inspired by stories of valor and people who use their personal stories to overcome. She is a "Jill of all Trades" and specializes in creative writing, communications, education, poetry, event planning, and the nonprofit sector. Please contact her at myjourneythroughwords@gmail.com for future writing opportunities.

SOURCES

CDC MMWR. (June 4, 2010, vol. 59) *Youth Risk Behavior Surveillance – United States, 2009.*

http://www.cdc.gov/mmwr/pdf/ss/ss5905.pdf (Accessed 10/25/2011)

Alliance for Excellent Education. *Education in the United States.*
http://www.all4ed.org/about_the_crisis/schools/map (accessed 10/25/2011)

http://www.all4ed.org/files/Arizona.pdf (accessed 10/25/2011) http://www.all4ed.org/files/NationalStates_seb.pdf (accessed 10/25/2011)

EPE Research Center/EdWeek Maps. *State Graduation Report.*
http://www.edweek.org/apps/gmap/details.html?year=2011&zoom=6&type=1&id=AZ (accessed 10/25/2011)

http://www.all4ed.org/files/HighSchoolDrop outs.pdf (Accessed 6/12/12)

CDC MMWR. (June 4, 2010, vol. 59) *Youth Risk Behavior Surveillance – United States, 2009.*

http://www.cdc.gov/mmwr/pdf/ss/ss5905.pdf (Accessed 10/25/2011)

http://www.guttmacher.org/pubs/FB-ATSRH.html (Accessed 06/12/12)

http://www.toonaripost.com/2012/05/us-news/poverty-striking-broken-homes-in-america/ (Accessed 06/12/12)

http://health.usnews.com/health-news/diet-fitness/diet/
    articles/2011/11/02/overweight-teens-dont-seem-to-grasp-weight-
    loss-rules (Accessed 11/2/11).
CDC MMWR. (June 4, 2010, vol. 59) *Youth Risk Behavior
    Surveillance – United States, 2009.*
http://www.cdc.gov/mmwr/pdf/ss/ss5905.pdf (Accessed 10/25/2011)
National Cancer Institute, *SEER Cancer Statistics Review 1975-2008,
    Updated October 20, 2011.* http://seer.cancer.gov/csr/1975_2008/
    results_merged/sect_28_childhood_cancer.pdf
(Accessed October 28, 2011)
http://www.donorschoose.org/blog/2011/02/15/teachers-vs-childhood-
    obesity/?gclid=CIr4tN-xybACFQZ5hwodA3KIVw (Accessed
    6/12/12).
Source: http://americanspcc.org/lp/bullying-01/
CDC Vital Signs. *Preventing Teen Pregnancy in the US.* http://www.cdc.
    gov/VitalSigns/pdf/2011-04-vitalsigns.pdf (accessed 10/24/2011)
Arizona Department of Health Services. *Teen Pregnancy and Birth in
    Arizona, 2010*
http://www.azdhs.gov/phs/owch/pdf/factSheets/TeenPregnancy-
    BirthArizona2010.pdf
http://azdhs.gov/phs/owch/pdf/issues/
    TeenPregnancyAndBirthInArizona2010.pdf (accessed 10/24/2011)
Alliance for Excellent Education. *Education in the United States.*
    http://www.all4ed.org/about_the_crisis/schools/map (accessed
    10/25/2011)
http://www.all4ed.org/files/Arizona.pdf (accessed 10/25/2011)
http://www.all4ed.org/files/NationalStates_seb.pdf (accessed
    10/25/2011)
EPE Research Center/EdWeek Maps. *State Graduation Report.*
http://www.edweek.org/apps/gmap/details.html?year=2011&zoom=6
    &type=1&id=AZ (accessed 10/25/2011)

http://www.myfoxdc.com/story/18600219/broken-homes-and-teen-parents-blamed-for-poor-social-mobility-in-uk-and-us (Accessed 6/12/12)

Change If I Can, You Can, is the first in a series of powerful books by Travis Angry designed to support his greater mission of helping youth and adults choose better lives for themselves. Look for the next book in his series, *Fighting to Serve*, coming soon. For more on his upcoming books and project, visit <u>TravisAngry.com</u>."

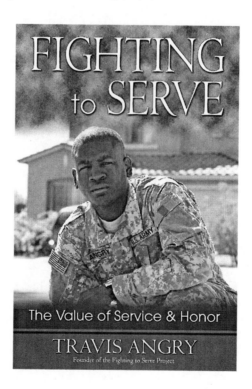

CPSIA information can be obtained at www.ICGtesting.com
Printed in the USA
LVOW10s0003100114

368858LV00015B/487/P

9 781614 486497